CUE
Cumbria

The County's Young People Write

editors:
Sandra Glover
Peter Mortimer

First published
November 2000 by IRON Press
5 Marden Terrace
Cullercoats
North Shields
Northumberland
NE30 4PD
UK
Tel/Fax: (0191) 253 1901
E-mail: seaboy@freenetname.co.uk
ISBN 0 906228 79 4
Printed by Tyneside Free Press, Newcastle upon Tyne

© This collection IRON Press 2000
© Individual items, The Authors and Artists 2000

Cover & Book Design by IRON Eye

IRON Press Books are distributed by
Signature Book Representation Ltd
Sun House
2, Little Peter St, Manchester M15 4PS UK
Tel: (0161) 834 8767 Fax: (0161) 834 8656
E-mail: admin@signature-books.co.uk

The main funders of **Cue Cumbria** are the **Cumberland Building Society**, which won an award from Arts & Business for its support of **Cue Cumbria**. Arts & Business is funded by the Arts Council of England and the Department for Culture. Media and Sport

Foreword

Writing in this anthology sprang from eight Cumbrian schools. In each school, a dozen pupils from years eight, nine and ten (covering ages 13-15) worked with a professional writer over a six months period. Each school had five full days of workshops, teachers being closely involved in most sessions.

The writers were the Cumbrian children's novelist Sandra Glover and the Tyneside playwright and poet Peter Mortimer, both of whom encouraged the pupils to pursue their own creative forms, and to experiment with the new. The idea was to nurture and encourage the young writers' individual talents, and expose them as much as possible to the rigours faced by professional authors.

Pupils from the schools also provided the artwork, and the writing was proof-read by the authors themselves. They were involved as much as possible in different aspects of production, from creating the words, to the book being on the bookshop shelf.

Space restrictions mean, that although many of the young writers were prolific, in the majority of cases, they are limited to one item apiece - more have been included where possible.

Several young writers were ambitious enough to tackle longer works, and in these cases were consulted as to which extract should be used.

The editors would like to thank the funders, especially Cumbria County Council, for the faith they showed in supporting the project.

Contents

- 7. Introductions
- 13. Poem: **Clare Mackay**
  Illus: **the Author**
- 14. poem: **Laura Waite**
- 15. The Teenage Years:
  Vincent Peart
- 16. Haiku: **Polly Smith**
- 17. Beetroot's Wedding:
  Beth Timson
- 20. True Story:
  Shirley-Anne Batey
- 21. Poem: **Lindsey Telfer**
- 22. Poem: **Hannah Trohear**
- 23. Poem: **Paul Moralee**
- 24. Alston Traditions:
  Nicola McGarr
  Illus: **Jessica Burt**
- 25. Poem:
  Anna-Alicia Parker
- 26. Poem: **James Alderson**
- 27. Poem: **Gemma McCowen**
- 28. A Strained Visit:
  Stephanie Roe
- 30. Two Poems: **Gemma Park**
  Illus: **Lisa Doran**
- 31. The Hangin' Place:
  Jennifer Boyd
- 32. Poem: **Katie Fairhall**
- 33. Haiku: **Alexander Stewart**
- 34. Little Langdale:
  Thomas Little
- 35. Haiku: **Gabrielle O'Connor**
- 36. Poem: **Claire Stewart**
  Illus: **Nicola Clorley**
- 37. Poem: **Claire Millican**
  Illus: **Nicola Clorley**
- 38. Toe-Nail Tiddlywinks:
  Jessica Anne Burt
- 39. Poem: **Davey Liddle**
  Haiku: **Martyn Metcalfe**
- 40. Haiku: **Kimberley Swinburne**
- 41. Poem: **Alice Horrocks**
- 42. Short Poem: **Claire Shaw**
- 43. Poem: **Michael Bottomley**
- 44. Think Yourself Lucky:
  Amy Lawrence
- 49. Poem: **Katie Stanton**
- 50. Poem: **Stewart Wardlaw**
- 51. Poem: **Gabrielle O'Connor**
- 52. Poem: **Philip Baxter**
- 53. Rainy Day Blues:
  Jayne Calvert
- 54. Poem: **Hannah Cleasby**
- 55. My Grandad Bert:
  Claire Shaw
- 56. Siblings: **Hannah Shepherd**
  Illus: **the Author**
- 58. Poem: **Jacki Best** and
  Polly Smith
- 59. Poem: **Craig Bell**
  Bath Time Noises:
  Thomas Swannick
- 60. Poem: **Rachel Thomas**
- 61. Two Poems:
  Claire Mattinson
- 62. Poem: **Martin Gallagher**
  Limerick: **Matthew Cannon**,
  Michael Bottomley and
  Ben Grigg
- 63. Millenium Frogs:
  Lynsey Galloway

64. Daily Brain Diet: **Roderick Allen**
65. Thoughts: **Mary-Anne Evison**
66. The Interview: **Michael Johnstone** Illus: **the Author**
68. Poem: **Paul Wren**
69. Poem: **Patrick Isherwood**
70. Jesus Found in Supermarket: **Ben Grigg**
71: Poem: **Jenny Kruger**
72: Not Even A Fig Leaf: **Beth Robinson** Illus: **Nicola Clorley**
74. Poem: **Rachel Grennell**
75. Excuses! Excuses!: **Nick Wright**
76. Poem: **Nicola Hall**
77. Poem: **Louise Wilson**
78. Poem: **Amy Symonds**
79. Poem: **Charlotte Liversidge** Illus: **Nicola Clorley**
80. Eternal Flame: **Ashley Iveson**
83: Sweet & Sour: **Emma Crowe**
85. Things They Seem to Like Doing: **Lynsey Jones** Illus: **Aimee Henry**
87: Poem: **Claire Stewart**
88. Betrayal: **John O'Connor**
89. Poem: **Amy Lawrence**
90. Paranoia & The Hippo: **Hannah Robinson** Illus: **Eleanor Wakefield**
91. the parti: **Kimberley Swinburne**
92. Poem: **Gavin Routledge**
93. Poem: **Roxanne Kliszat**
94. Poem: **Stefenie Anderson** Illus: **Nicola Clorley**
95. The Baby Vampire: **Rachel McAlone**
97. Recipe for a Perfect Day: **Gemma Staunton**
98. Ivan Idea: **Hannah Robinson**
99. Lost & Found: **Caroline Haigh**
100. Poem: **Laura Robson**
101. Santa's Letter: **Thomas Prince**
102. Beginnings: **Toby Hine**
104. Short Poem: **Hannah Shepherd**
105. Experimental: **Amy Wakefield**
106. Poem: **Toni Gilmore** Illus: **the Author**
107. Poem: **Tom Swannick**
108. Life is a River: **Mary-Anne Evison**
109. The Over-Enthusiastic Dad: **Louise Bell**
110. Mismatch: **Aimee Henry**
111. Granny's Shopping List: **Elizabeth Fye** Illus: **Lisa Doran**
114. Poem: **Alexander Stewart**
115. RIP (Maybe): **Imogen McGarvie**
116. Two Poems: **Tom Smith**
117. Fish Wish: **Martyn Metcalfe** Illus: **the Author**
120. Generation: **Natalie Craig**

122. Poem: **Paula Price**
123. Poem: **Beth Dodd**
124. Poem: **Jessica Thompson**
125. The Lost Painting:
     Caroline Eden
126. Poem: **Beth Robinson**
     Illus: **the Author**
127. Lonely Sultan:
     Matthew Cannon
128. Poem: **Sarah Mannix**
129. Poem:
     Shirley-Anne Batey
     Illus: **Polly Smith**
130. Poem: **Elaine Capstick**
     Poem: **Stewart Wardlaw**
131. Friends So Far:
     Samantha Tatters
133. The Founder of the Name Wigton:
     Eleanor Wakefield
134. Poem: **Kimberely Waite**
     Illus: **Nicola Clorley**
135. Poem: **James Kirby**
     Illus: **the Author**
136. Dead Man's Party:
     Terri McCrickerd
137. Poem: **Stefenie Anderson**
138. Poem: **Amy Henderson**
139. Poem: **Jo Sedgwick**
140. A Conflict of Powers:
     Steven Gibson
142. Poem: **Paul Wren**
143. Poem: **Lisa Doran**
144. Poem:
     Joanna Mottershead
145. Poem: **Claire Mattinson**

147. **The New Dictionary**:
     The Lingo of Tomorrow!

The Cumbrian Schools which took part in **Cue Cumbria** are:

Alfred Barrow School, Barrow-in-Furness
John Ruskin School, Coniston
Nelson Thomlinson School, Wigton
St. Aidan's County High School, Carlisle
St. Joseph's RC High School, Workington
Samuel King's School, Alston
Settlebeck High School, Sedbergh
Whitehaven School, Whitehaven

Introduction One

Education is an increasingly stressful business - for both teachers and pupils alike. The former often find the burden of the job intolerable and rush for early retirement, while the latter have been known to smash up the furniture, turn to arson or incite violence.
We begin to wonder what it is all for, and who (or what) does it produce. There are no easy answers. Nor does it do much good to hark back to a mythical golden age where innocent youngsters were tucked in with a mug of hot cocoa and an Enid Blyton. There was no golden age.
It's true that with the advent of computers, the play station etc, young people read less. The printed book has often prematurely been pronounced dead, just as the public cinema was pronounced dead when videos took the world by storm.
Cinema attendances have rocketed of late.
Human beings regularly confound the doom merchants -as does this collection. It is a testament to young people's willingness to engage creatively in the written word. A writer working in a school can sometimes feel in alien territory. Here are large institutions going about the serious business of getting people through examinations. And here is a writer, often working on hunch or instinct rather than logic, tempted maybe by the playful, encouraging spontaneity or the unpredictable, knowing the value of the random, or, as Eliot put it, "*When a poet's mind is perfectly equipped for its work, it is constantly amalgamating disparate experience.*" Like many writers, I've at times stood in a classroom and felt a silent hostility from some quarters - suggesting my attempts to undermine the education system were viewed with less than total admiration. And a project such as *Cue Cumbria* isn't

easy- for the writers, the pupils, the teachers, the schools. Normal rules don't apply. There are no marks, no exams, no right or wrong answers, no body of information handed *en masse* from the 'educator' to the 'educatee'. The writer should learn as much from the excercise as anyone.

When I first walk into a classroom I have little idea what will happen next. This scares me stiff, but doing it any other way proves sterile. The outcome depends greatly on the chemistry of everyone in that particular room.

In my four schools in Alston, Workington, Whitehaven and Wigton, many of us often struggled hard. I felt some pupils at times were on the brink of giving up. The idea had been to subject them as much as possible to the demands faced by professional writers. But we also intended to have a lot of fun and ultimately we did, at times acting spontaneously, such as when we fled the building for sudden *haiku walks*.

The young writers inched their way forward, attempting not only the expected poetry and prose forms, but also film and TV scripts, cartoons, song lyrics, snippets of things. We created a dictionary of new words. At the start of the sessions, each group was told no-one was guaranteed publication. Later on Sandra and I agreed it would be heartless to exclude any young scribbler after such lengthy determination. Even so, the editing of the book involved a good deal of selection and reselection.

Each group I was involved in had its own dynamics. Some set off like a train and then slowed. Others were more cautious starters, late flowerers. What I found heartening was how each group was mature enough to take on board the business of writing, that demanding, mainly solitary, but ultimately rewarding business. Imagine their delight to see their names and work in this book.

Nor was it easy for the schools, taking pupils off the ever-demanding syllabus. Teachers were encouraged to participate in the workshops, and, in the main, did.

Teaching is one of the hardest, and without doubt the

most important profession. The best schools are the ones where you feel a sense of excitement, adventure, challenge, where, despite the demands and strictures, young minds are still valued and nurtured as more than just exam fodder, the process seen as more than just passport to a job. In the worst schools there is the sense of daily drudge, a head-down, often cynical approach of just getting through it. The attitude of any school staff filters its way through to the pupils, just as these pupils and their attitudes eventually filter into the world at large.

In its own small way, I hope this book, which the former Literature Development Agency for Cumbria County Council, ALL WRITE! was instrumental in bringing about, emphasises the importance of diversity in our education system, giving young minds on occasions the chance to roam free, unfettered. I often felt really close to and supportive of my four groups, and I am proud to be associated with their work in print. Their workshop days were stretched over a long period, needing stamina, resilience and imagination. I think they've produced some smashing work.

I'd also like to pay tribute to those teachers who were brave enough to take part in the process. It was an invasion of their territory. It was their own procedures which often had to be laid aside. But their support, participation and good humour was a vital part of the process.

Grateful thanks also to Stephanie Simm of Cumbria Arts in Education whose support and good humour helped carry us through the more prickly moments.

Enough of that! Enjoy what is to come, and watch out for some of these names in the future. You might see one nominated for the Whitbread or the Booker Award.

Peter Mortimer
Cullercoats,
Summer 2000

Introduction Two

When I moved to Cumbria in 1998, friends were quick to point out how fortunate I was. They meant, quite rightly, the chance to live in such a beautiful county, surrounded by hills, lakes and glorious countryside. All of which I greatly appreciate.

But there was more. In Cumbria I found a county actively engaged in the promotion of writing and indeed, all the creative arts.

As soon as I read about the *Cue Cumbria* project, I knew it was something I wanted to be iinvolved in. Unlike Peter, schools are familiar enough territory for me. I was a teacher for fifteen years even before I started to write, so the project was a chance to combine my passion for creative writing with my love of working with young people.

I wasn't disappointed. The pupils and staff at Alfred Barrow, John Ruskin, Settlebeck, and St.Aidan's were a delight to work with.

Immediately impressive was the fact that many of the pupils were already committed writers, full of ideas, developing their own styles, and keen to show me the collections of their work. Other pupils were less confident, some expressing doubts about their ability to write anything at all.

During the workshops we used a variety of sources to help generate ideas. We looked at pictures, listened to music, played word games, thought about personal experiences, created bizarre characters, read and talked.

A variety of work began to emerge as pupils responded in their unique ways. From the same starting point in a workshop might come prose, poems or dialogue, real life dramas or pure fantasy, zany humour or serious, thoughtful pieces.

Feedback was an important part of each session. Pupils were encouraged to share their work with friends or read it out to the whole group, where they offered each other support, and gentle criticism, with amazing maturity and increasing confidence. As news of their excellent work began to filter round the schools, teachers and head teachers joined the reading sessions, offering their own encouragement and praise.

Part of the final session in each school involved pupils working in groups, re-reading their pieces and selecting their favourites. Even some of the pupils who told me they weren't very good at writing found that they had produced several impressive pieces and that it was difficult to choose!

Still more difficult for Peter and myself was selecting just one main piece per pupil to include in the book. We actually managed to squeeze in a few extra short pieces. I think the result is one that the schools and pupils can be proud of.

The project was demanding for everyone. The schools were tolerant of disruption to routine and very supportive. The pupils worked hard, stretching their creativity to the limit, engaging in the task of drafting and rewriting pieces. They learnt to cope with disappointment when a particular piece didn't work out, but also gained tremendous satisfaction and confidence from those which did. I hope they also had fun and enjoyed the experience. I know I did.

I hope too that they will feel inspired to continue writing. Like Peter, I feel I may well have worked with young writers who we will be hearing more of in the future

Sandra Glover
Milton, Cumbria,
Summer 2000.

This book is dedicated to Anne Horrocks
1946-1999

Mrs. Horrocks was a teacher at
St. Joseph's R.C.High School,
Workington who worked closely
with Peter Mortimer. She had
a lovely sense of humour and
was very generous with her time,
both to the writing group, and
other events.
She will be sadly missed.

St.Joseph's Writing Group

Cue Cumbria

10 reasons for not handing in your homework!!!

Clare Mackay (St.Joseph's)

1. .My brother sneezed on it and I didn't want to infect the school with germs.

2. I did it so well that somebody stole it to copy.

3. I used it to wrap your Christmas present.

4. I wanted to protect the environment and couldn't find any recycled paper.

5. My hand was in plaster and my left hand had gout.

6. My doctor says that homework is wearing out my brain.

7. I was visiting my great aunt who lives on the moon and my homework floated away. It's probably orbiting Jupiter by now

8. I gave it to a third world child in another country to read because they can't afford books.

9. My mum borrowed it for the baby because we ran out of nappies

10. What homework....?

Cue Cumbria

Recipe for annoying teachers

Laura Waite
(Alfred Barrow)

Ingredients

1	Small stuffy classroom
10	Screamy children
	Equipment flying everywhere
4	Pupils without homework
2	Throwing things
2	Fighting
2	Chewing

Take 1 stuffy classroom. Carefully add 10 screamy children mixed with a big, fat, moany teacher. Stir them all together so the party gets going.
Beat in 4 children without homework; 2 throwing things; 2 fighting and 2 chewing. Keep on whisking until the teacher is heated up nicely.
When the teacher begins to cool down re-heat quickly with 3 pupils demanding to go to the loo.
Allow to settle.
As everyone begins to cool down, slice in more children, until the room starts to boil and the paint begins to peel!
While the trouble's still bubbling, the teacher's on fire, and the children are chilling, whisk in the head.

The Teenage Years

**Vincent Peart
(Samuel King's)**

Adolescence, the coming, like a caterpillar emerging into a butterfly. For some the best days of their lives, for others their worst. Up to the age of twelve we are seen as children too innocent to cause trouble and too sweet to be a menace. Over the age of eighteen we are seen as adults, too responsible to cause trouble and too wise to be looked down on.

The teenage years are strange; fuelled by hormones, alcohol, loud music, love, cigarettes, drugs, films and videogames. (The teenager marches on). We sit on street corners because there is nothing else to do; television rots your brain, homework is too boring and the council closed down our youth club. When we meet our friends, older people see us as a threat, when in reality we mean no harm. Our loud music, stupid games and knocking on doors is seen as terrorising the community and not as the lighthearted fun it really is.

Many teenagers smoke in a rural community; starting out of boredom. A quick smoke is risky, even dangerous, and it wastes ten minutes of an empty day Then one day they will try to go without a cigarette and they realise they can't, and so become hooked. Another drug linked to us is alcohol. Cheap bottles of cider are freely available, drinking is something to do. It makes the night more fun and you can socialise better, do stupid things and have a laugh.

There is a link between all of the teenagers' habits and boredom. There is nothing for us and so we have to do something with our monotonous lives. The boredom leads to laziness and you can't be bothered to do homework, there is no motivation or encouragement to do well. We do not have enough money to do anything that has a price and so that leads the most desperate of us to cause crime.

People say "get a job" but at our age jobs are either too hard work or too poorly paid, pocket money helps but only just, this leads some of us to steal and shoplift, not out of hatred or contempt for the owner, just for some extra money to get by.

Some teenagers may take drugs and fair enough; it is their choice. But their friends should not be seen as junkies because they know someone who takes drugs. It is unfair and unjustified.

In short do not judge me by the actions of others, do not tell me how to live my life, take care of your own life and stop worrying about others.

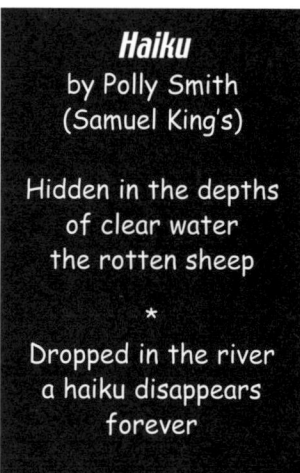

Haiku
by Polly Smith
(Samuel King's)

Hidden in the depths
of clear water
the rotten sheep

*

Dropped in the river
a haiku disappears
forever

Cue Cumbria

Beetroot's Wedding

Beth Timson
(Settlebeck)

Princess Gherkin looked down at her feet. The old, worn-out trainers that were now made out of lanky old string were standing on a long stretch of puddly concrete. There was, right at the bottom of the back yard, a bit of grass with a small flowerbed along one side, but it was so small that by the time you actually reached it, there wasn't much that you could do with it. Like everything else in the Royal household it looked as if it were long past its sell-by date. She stared up at her goal, the gate at the bottom of the garden, and picked up the heavy bag of rubbish.

"Well, it's taking out the rubbish time again and there at the starting blocks we can see Miss Gherkin Snothankyou trying to beat her personal best of..um...ah well, you know getting there and back" said the voice of the crackly loud-speaker in her mind.

"Here we go, on your marks, get set, GO! "
Gherkin shot off down the garden. When I say shot off I should really say *tried* to shoot off, but because of her trailing laces and the heavy bag, she didn't go very fast.
When Gherkin got back to the house she went straight up to the landing and sat down outside her sister's room where she had been keeping an overnight vigil. This was because about fifteen minutes before, she had been told that for her sister's wedding she would have to wear a luminous green dress. Of course it would go with the Barbie pink wedding dress and the luminous yellow of the aisle carpet, but she refused to be ridiculed in front of the nation.
Even now that the Royal family no longer got paid more than the average person on the dole they still had to let film crews in on the wedding. Tomorrow was to be the big day and

aside from that there was Gherkin's 13th birthday. She wasn't excited because there wasn't going to be any celebration for her, as all attention would be focussed on her sister. Now before I go any further, I must tell you a little about the Royal family. There is of course Gherkin, but there is also her sister Beetroot and her parents. Her dad was the typical couch potato with a beer belly and was always slouched in the chair with a few cans of lager next to him. He was married to his second wife at the time, who was Gherkin's real mother making Beetroot her half-sister. Her mother was the typical couch potato's wife. She was the one in the household who managed the money, and she was the one who spent most of it. She smoked, spent a lot of time down the pub and used King Prong hair dye.

Gherkin sat there listening to the designer and the hairdresser who had sneaked into Beetroot's bedroom while she had been doing her chores. Oh well, so much for the overnight vigil, but if she had refused to do her chores, her mother would have made her tidy the front room and that was definitely a bad punishment. Her mother never tidied up and that meant that the fag ends, beer cans and stale TV dinner cases littered the room like the covering of dead leaves on a forest floor.

The next day Gherkin sat on her bed in the notorious dress having her hair done by the world famous hairdresser Charlie Porksnip. So you would think that apart from the dress, Gherkin would be happy. But then, if you knew what the hairstyle looked like, you wouldn't. Charlie, the sponsor of King Prong, was very keen to get it some publicity
and had done her hair in purple and yellow spikes.

"You look lovely darling. I'm sure then whole nation will be amazed!" was the inevitable response from her mother. "I mean, that dress will be the talk of the town for ages!"

"Yes, it will be the talk of the town but only because it looks so ridiculous."

Gherkin looked away from her mother and sulked, In the car, on the way to church, Gherkin felt this was going to be the worst day of her life especially as the heart throb Paul Pimple would be there looking at her in all her finery.

In the church, as Gherkin stood behind her sister, she felt as if she were about to enter the unknown .From here she could see Paul Pimple and the nerves were flying around like donkeys. Well, have you ever seen nerves fly?

The wedding was soon over and the bright red blush on Gherkin's face said it all really. She hadn't done anything wrong but it was what she had been meant to do right that was the problem. Her sister's tastes , although in keeping whith the rest of the family, were absolutely dreadful. She had made her poor sister get up and make a fool of herself by singing a specially composed song.

"On this day of love and mirth,
we herald this time of birth,
The great birth of this marriage,
Let's see them roll off in a horse and carriage."

This was turning out to be one of the most embarrassing days of her life and what's more Paul Pimple had been on the front pew with the best view of the whole church. Gherkin flounced across the church yard and, not caring how ripped her dress got, she climbed up the apple trees with ease. Fifteen minutes later she was woken by voices below her.

"I feel so sorry for her though. "
It was Paul Pimple on the bench beneath her! Great thought Gherkin, that's all I need but she had no choice but to listen to the rest of the conversation.

"How would you like to dress like that for your sister's wedding *and* it was broadcast on T.V. How embarrassing." Paul's friend nodded and was about to speak but Paul carried on.

"I had to dress totally stupid for uncle Barry's wedding but the photos of that mysteriously disappeared when I slept at his house."

"You've got a bit of a soft spot for Gherkin haven't you?" said the friend with a sly smile on his face. Paul looked at him.

"*Of course* I do." Gherkin gasped with delight and lent backwards. Pimple found Gherkin in his lap.

"Did you......"

"I like you too." Gherkin smiled as he lent forward to kiss her.

True Story
by Shirley-Anne Batey
(Samuel King's)

Friday night mam and dad went to a dance. They sent me to stay with my uncle for the night while they went out. The next day I went to work and mam and dad walked in. Mam pulled me aside and told me she and dad got married. I was so shocked, also upset, wondering why they didn't tell me that they were going to do it. Yesterday I was a Smith, now I'm a Batey.

Where I belong

Lindsey Telfer
(Settlebeck)

Times Square, New York
a badminton court
Melbourne, Australia
on top of Winder

Power and exhiliration,
adrenalin, fast moving,
different races, different people

Farrers coffee shop
in bed
friends' houses

Security and comfort
warmth and sagging sofas
the girlie chats, the knowingness.

America, with the cast of *Dawson's Creek*
dreams

Speechless, in awe
be anybody, anywhere,
options open, new feelings.

Two Poems

Hannah Trohear
(St.Joseph's)

Morning Child

Where have all the stars and moon gone?
They were there when I went to bed.
Do they sleep through the morning?
Have they gone to school instead?
Did they have an argument?
Or did they fall into the sea?
Maybe they exploded into diamonds of light.
Will they ever come back to me?

Haiku

In the window pane
the outside world
quivers in reflection
*
The nettle is waiting
for the passing
flesh
*
The emerald ivy
grips the tree
climbing steadily
*
The autumn leaves fade
dirt and mud
trampled over them

The Overweight Hamster

Paul Moralee (St. Aidan's)

Ooo, look food.
Boy do those kids overfeed me!
I'm so fat
I've got a specially made cage.
But,
Ha, ha
I still want to escape
I've still got my ambition and drive
I want to find a mate,
Have lots of little hamsters,
Live happily ever after.
Soooo
I've got to go on a diet
Get thin
Exercise
Go for more runs round my wheel,
do press ups,
sharpen my teeth
Eat Healthily,
But...
Not today
Tomorrow.
Ooo look food!

Alston Traditions

Cue Cumbria

Nicola McGarr
(Samuel King's)

The ancient Alstonian tradition of naked Morris Dancing takes place on the 3rd day of the 7th month at 9.36pm. Four local youths are chained to a pole in the middle of the foundry. They begin to chant and wave a large silver wand in the air, trying to make contact with Waptap the God of dance and movement.

To join in the festivities, the contestants must go through a series of tasks, naked of course, including leap frog, high jump and break dancing. A final jousting match will determine who will get to be one of the next troop of dancers.

The annual tradition was founded by a local one-armed squirrel protector called Pete. One day he decided to be at one with nature and take all his clothing off. He was so happy to be free of his dirty green mac, that he decided to dance around a fence post in the middle of the Firs walk. The great idea of naked Morris Dancing was born!

The event has been taking place ever since.

Blue Is

Anna-Alicia Parker (Alfred Barrow)

Blue is the lake, river, or sea
Blue is the word, deprived of its glee
Blue is the whale, big and strong
Blue is the shark with the fish long gone
Blue is the eyes happy and shining
Blue is the tear, falling and glistening
Blue is the flower with the calming bell
Blue is the rain that forever fell
Blue is a bright primary colour
Blue is my mind, never fuller
Blue is the sky, clouds and all
Blue is my heart frozen and small.

Buckets of Heat

James Alderson
(Samuel King's)

They were locked in
couldn't move.
Darkness surrounded them.
The blanket of night enveloped the air they breathed.
Sharp metallic sounds whistled through the air
Screams were not welcome,
They increased the tension.
A monotonous tone could be heard as the snake within its skin coiled and contracted,
Its victims screamed and screamed
Sweat poured down their skin.
Bucket loads of heat pressured them into eventual submission,
"HELP, HELP!"
They cried.
Sudden salvation.

The ghost train ends

What a Ride

Gemma McCowen
(Alfred Barrow)

They said I'd get a rush.
"No, I don't like heights."
They said they'd pay...
So up up up,
The carriage rattled like a baby's toy
Up the wooden track.
I held on tight
my fingers white.
Eyes shut
Stomach churning
Muscles burning
Slowly one eye opens
Amazing sight
People rushing around
The ground.
Feel the fear
Wind rushing at my face
Body loosening
Breath snatched
Screeching wheels
"Guess what
You owe me a fiver!"
Before I faint.

Cue Cumbria

A Strained Visit

Stephanie Roe
(St.Joseph's)

(Scene: The doctor's surgery.)

Doctor   Right, so what seems to be the problem?

Patient   What do you mean? Can't you see, can't you tell?

Doctor   What have your symptoms been?

Patient   What do you mean, my symptoms! Are you blind? Look at me, is it not obvious what's wrong with me!

Doctor   It looks to me like a case of a runny nose.

Patient   A runny nose! How can you say I have a runny nose?

Doctor   If you go to bed with a hot water bottle and plenty of tissue,s it'll clear up right away.

Patient   Clear up! Look doctor, don't you understand, this won't clear up - I'm a teabag!

Doctor   You should also try to keep warm. You'll have to be very careful this doesn't become worse.

Patient   How can this become worse, aren't you listening to me or looking at me. Yesterday I was a human being and today I'm a teabag!

Doctor	Take two of these tablets twice a day and you should be fine.
Patient	Look I haven't got a runny nose I'm a ruddy six foot tall tea bag.
Doctor	We'll need you to come back in a week and we'll take another look but you should be fine.
Patient	In a week! You want me to spend another week as a Tetley teabag!
Doctor	I'll see you next week. In the meantime try not to spread that runny nose! Could you send the next person in please. Thank you.

Two Poems

Gemma Park (St. Joseph's)

The Man in the Trunk

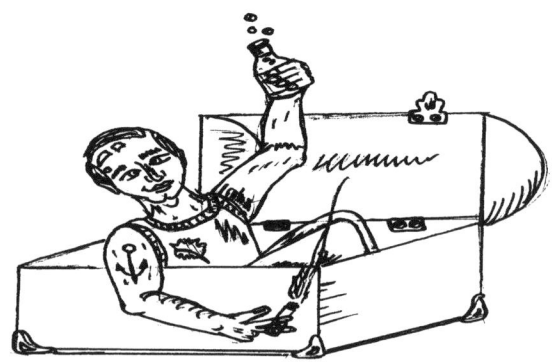

There was an old man in a trunk
Who asked of his wife,"Am I drunk"?
She replied with regret,

"I'm afraid so my pet"
And he answered "it's just as I think."

My Granny.

My granny sits at home all day,
Staring at fish and flowers.
Then at night she flips her wig,
and goes down the pub for hours.

The 'Hangin' Place'.

Jennifer Boyd (St.Aidan's)

We're alway here. All my free time is spent on this empty car park, next to the old flats. It's totally deserted like a desert with only the sand to call its friend, but yet our gang loves hangin' on the hangin' place.

We even sometimes like to bunk off school but not all the time. It's not exactly Ibiza, Majorca or even Benidorm - but we still have a laugh.
If my mum caught me she'd kill me like a cheetah killing its prey. I'm already in enough trouble as it is. One more step out of line and she'll probably disown me.

In our family there's me, mum and my five, trouble making, rat faced brothers and sisters. A bit overcrowded if you ask me. Seven of us in a three bedroomed council house. How blissful! That's why I quite like going to the car park, to hang out at the Hangin' place.

Cue Cumbria

Caged

Katie Fairhall
(Whitehaven)

With the monotonous plodding of my paws
every day is the same
the human beings have arrived
fat ones, thin ones, small ones, tall ones
they come in different sizes
some have spots and long curly hair
some have buttoned noses with gleaming smiles
old ones hobble along with their walking sticks
whilst young ones run and make a mess
they scream laugh and run
throwing things at my head
and trying to be funny, roaring just like me
they munch away on food
dropping ice cream everywhere
and the litter is revolting
there is a mountain growing outside my lair
there are crisp packets and chewing gum stuck firmly to the ground
mars bars and chewitt wrappers and
cigarette butts and lollipop sticks are all adding to the pile
I turn to face them
and bare my impressive teeth
I growl a little, quite fiercely
but they just snigger and turn away
I want it like before
when I was in my African land
At home there wasn't an horizon
I could run wherever I liked
go and drink from the shaded water hole
or sleep in the warm dry sun

Now I'm caged without a life
there I was, King of the pride,
admired by all the rest, my huge crown made me in charge
but now the humans laugh at my hairy head
and my lovely lashing tail
they push their annoying hands into my cage
I loudly roar and dart for their skinny fingers
the one thing I wait for in every day.

Haiku
by Alexander Stewart
(St. Joseph's)

Trees in the wind
wounded
without fighting

*

The cow
watches the boy
chewing his gum

Cue Cumbria

The Tale of Little Langdale and its Sheep

Thomas Little
(St. Aidan's)

One day a group of unwilling school children, from a small northern city, went on an evil, eerie, dangerous trip with dangerous teachers or what they thought were teachers! The day began when the poor souls arrived at the school building. They stood outside for a ridiculous amount of time until the teachers realised that twelve cups of coffee was too much in one morning. So they loaded the kids into the bus with the psychotic driver who thought that breathing in affected the width of the bus! They eventually reached the hell hole that is LITTLE LANGDALE! A kind of outdoor activities centre, run by the school , where the unlucky kids go , to have fun and enjoy the country side. But there was something twisted and eerie about the place that you will learn of during our tale. Anyway when the gang arrived they shot up stairs towards the so called dormitories where only the lowest forms of life, such as the writers of East Enders and those old puppets from Playdays go. They argued for a while over who should get which bed and explained to the new kid how some girl hung herself, before finally settling for the night. Everything was going fine for 3 days until..........

Wednesday night when the group went outdoors to spend the night in the open. They played pointless games involving putting spirit and ash on their faces, built some tents out of bin liners and sat round the fire. They told ghost stories. Then one boy sitting at the back said "Did you hear that?" "What?" the rest screamed!

"I don't know, I think it was a sheep, but its coming closer" "It's probably nothing" said Mr Boy, the teacher with them."Oh no" said another voice at the back. "Don't you

remember? It's the robotic sheep Thomas Little used to tell us about until he was killed when he wrestled with that grizzly bear."
The others sat terrified. Then out of the darkness came a whole army of metal sheep.
The kids screamed, so did the teachers. Then one boy was set alight by one of the sheep. He ran around screaming until he dropped dead.
Some farmers heard the screams but when they got there....
ASHES!!!!!!!

Haiku
by Gabrielle O'Connor
(St.Joseph's)

In the cold wind
two blackbirds
sing a song
*
The old couple
hand in hand
down the quiet path

Fire

Claire Stewart (Nelson Thomlinson)

A curving, coiling, hypnotic seducer
I kiss my aura with drawling tongues,
A glowing silhouette of Medusa,
Breathing slow sighs from black-hot lungs

I'm a torn temptress whispering silent lies,
In a saffron ragged silk attire,
In opium-like hazes lurk my swaying snake eyes,
They flow and ebb with beats of tremulous desire.

I'm the witch's charm weaver,
I'm Lucifer's eternal goddess,
I can rage or smite with sweltering fever,
or scowl in sulking moodiness,
I can blaze an inferno with a spiteful roar,
or scorch, blast and torch 'till life's no more.

Radiant in dark, my ochre glows,
As I dance on my wax throne,
But as easy as I can see the life into your soul,
I could char and blacken your pearly bone.

Some People Say I'm Mad

Claire Millican (Nelson Thomlinson)

Some people say I'm mad.
They say:
"The lights are on but nobody's home";
"The engines running but there's no-one behind the wheel";
They ask if I'm all right upstairs.
They say I'm:
Loony;
Dotty;
Dopey;
Potty.
Tell me I'm a whisky glass short of an alcoholic;
A French-fry short of a Big-Mac;
A tube of Pringles short of a French trip;
A daffodil short of a space ship!

Toe-nail Tiddlywinks

Cue Cumbria

Jessica Anne Burt.
(Samuel King's)

In Alston the ancient ritual of toe-nail tiddlewinks is celebrated at Fairhill park on the 10th day of every 3rd month - this enables the toe-nails to grow to their full potential. The weather must be cloudy as the sun could reflect off the clippers and ruin a contestant's chances. It must not be rainy as a slip of the clippers could end in disaster!

Contestants line up around the tennis court stretching and oiling their clippers. They stand about 3 metres away from the wall and aim at the small holes in the breezeblock with metre lines leading up to see the range of each clipping. Most people use the method known as "direct hit" which is aiming straight ahead of the hole. The other way is called "obliquing" which is aiming diagonally at the hole. Both methods are used.

The winner is the person who gets the most clippings in or close to the hole. He or she wins a trophy which is made out of the winners' nails stuck together.

This celebration originated on one rainy Gala day, when the barefooted "It's a knockout" contestants got bored and started picking their toe-nails and, for a laugh, aimed them at a bucket.

S'poze

Davey Liddle (St Aidan's)

Spoze if the world woz a big red jelly bean with sugar houses.
The roads were made of ice cream
and the pavement woz,
Made of big squishy 10p cola bottles.
Mmmmmm, yummy!
Paul-ize men run after robbers with their toy guns.
Those paul-ize mus' be dead fast to catch
All the big scary chocolate monsters were put in jails
Made of chocolate biscuits.
Oh! but we'd have to clean our teeth
10 millionsquillion times more!
Well, at least we'd never be 'ungry.

Haiku
by Martyn Metcalfe
(St.Joseph's)

In the winter air
the people smoke
without knowing

*

In the distance
the windmills
spin off their heads

Haiku

Kimberley Swinburne (St.Joseph's)

The sound of birds
fill the air
invisible to the eye

    *

Sheltering under the willow
the sun
peeping through the leaves

    *

The graffiti lamp post
tells stories
of past lovers

It's Just a Job

Alice Horrocks (Samuel King's)

Talking
Ignoring my presence
Slagging him off
As if he's not my dad.

Trying to impress
Telling their friends
Joking around
About the things he does in his job.

Calling him names
Doing impressions
With no idea I'm there
But they wouldn't care.

They see me now
Trying to suck up
Being all nice
And making me cringe.

"Ignore them" I think
They are pathetic as usual
Not understanding my point of view,
Or his.

It's his job,
Just a job.
Nothing wrong with that
So I thought.
They do it on the sly

They think I don't know
Whispering on the back of the bus
They must think I'm deaf.
Talking
Ignoring my presence
Slagging him off
As if he's not my dad
Just a teacher

Short Poem
by Claire Shaw
(Alfred Barrow)

I hate early mornings, when everything is hurried.
Oh, why can't mornings be after lunch?
Then I wouldn't feel so worried.

Death. Com. Life

Michael Bottomley (John Ruskin)

Death,
Wanderer of the earth,
Keeper of the dark side,
A rogue of souls

Death,
Longing for freedom
waiting for an absolution
To end our lonely suffering.

Technology,
An answer to a persistent problem,
A key within a possibility
A chance to walk the earth for endless years

DNA
A complexity within a complexity
A mystery within a mystery
A solution with technology.

Immortality
A goal for mankind
An unforseeable gift
An antidote of genetics
A crusher of extinction

Why would we want this?
Why dream of an eternity of possible chaos
Would you?

Cue Cumbria

"Think Yourself Lucky"

Amy Lawrence
(Whitehaven)

"Oh for God's sake! Why can't I get that new computer game? Everyone else has got one!"

"No you can't. We're not made of money".
Jessica sighed. Her mother wouldn't let her have *anything*. It was always the same excuses."We're not made of money"..."You just bought a new whatever"....or, one of the most popular,, "In my day..". It was so unfair!

Jessica couldn't be bothered listening to her mother's whining. Her attention wandered to the television. A mobile phone advertisement had come on. Mobiles were the in-thing of the moment. Jessica's eyes lit up- she would love to have one - so grown-up and fashionable!

"Mum, can I have a -"
"No, you can't have a mobile 'phone." "Honestly, it's just want, want, want!." :"In my day..."
Off she went again.
"But, mum, I need one!"
"You don't need anything! When you got that dress you apparently needed, you wore it only once. When you got that television for your room you desperately needed, you never used it. You watch telly down here and argue over the bloody remote!"

"But mum, this is different-"
"No it isn't. Anyway, I've just paid for you to go to France with the school!". Jessica groaned, annoyed. She was losing this argument and she knew it.

That's it. I've had enough, she thought. I need to make a quick exit before she goes on any more.

"Can I use the 'phone?"
"No, you can't. You spend far too long on that 'phone. Our

bills are far too high, We might as well throw our money down the drain! Why don't you walk and speak to her in person?"

"I want to ask her something. I'll only be a few minutes".

"You say that every time. A few minutes turns into ten, those ten stretch to half an hour, and you'll chat for ages. Go on, you need the exercise!"

"You don't let me do anything. Why couldn't I have been born somewhere else with loving kind parents?"

By now the adverts were over and the news had come on. There were reports of yet another devastating bombing in Kosovo, there were pictures of a refugee camp. Very young children had been separated from their parents. Their houses had burned down, many people had died.

Jessica walked out and slammed the lounge door. She picked up a bag of crisps en route. She just *had* to get away from her mother from hell. Halfway down the street Jessica stopped dead. She felt really peculiar. Her head was spinning, the houses were just a blur, and her body went limp as she fell to the ground. She blacked out. The next time she opened her eyes she could hear the screams of two tiny children.

"Mummy, mummy!" There was smoke! There was fire!

"Wake up dear child, the Serbs have attacked!"

Who? A shudder ran through her. The Serbs were talked about on the news. Something to do with ethnic cleansing. Jessica leapt out of bed. The screams got louder as the fire spread. They had to get out somehow. The door was blocked. The smoke was getting thicker. There was no way out. Wait a minute. The window. The household and herself were not far up. They could get out easily - all five of them. There was the mother, father, two children and herself. One by one they escaped through the window, and luckily got away with only a few bruises. They were a reasonable distance from the house when they turned round and watched in horror as the remains of the house burned down into a pile of ash.

The family and Jessica (by now somehow, she was part of the family) had to sort out what to do. They had no money, no clothes, and no shelter. They had one choice - to flee the country,

They began the long journey to the border. They travelled through the night and became hungrier and thirstier. They had to stay alert at all times. If the Serbs found them, they would be killed. Miraculously, within 24 hours, all five made it to the border, but were not allowed past.

"A day of travelling and for what?" they murmured sadly. "For absolutely nothing". Jessica sighed a breath of relief as a battered British Red Cross van caught her eye. She ran over.

"Excuse me, but that family over there needs help!"

"Sorry miss, the van's ful."

"Please sir, we've travelled all night. They'll die without help."

"If you don't mind me asking, what's a Brit kid like you doing here?"

"Erm - it's a long story."

"OK, I suppose we could fit a few more on."

They were loaded onto a van with other suffering people, many of whom had lost their families. An hour or so later they arrived. The place was an absolute dump. No running water, no paths, just a row of tents.

Life on the refugee camp was hard. There was food and

water, but not enough, and it wasn't particularly fresh. Every now and again the children would be lucky enough to get paper and pens, and drew pictures of their house and family before all the hatred and evil started. Hygiene was poor, there was little soap, no electricity, no telly, lighting. radio, nothing we take for granted in Britain.

Jessica lived there for days. How would she get back home? What would her parents be thinking? One day she discovered the packet of crisps from home. She was starving. She was about to take a bite, but stopped herself. She woke her 'family'. They got really excited when they saw the crisps. Their faces lit up. They offered Jessica one and when she said no, looked at her as if she was mad.

The next disaster struck. The Serbs attacked the camp. Tents were set alight. People were shot. Supplies were stolen.

Jessica found herself standing in the same place she had fallen before. It seemed brilliant. Decent shelter, electricity, decent life. She ran home. Her mother would be worried to bits! She must have been gone a week! Jessica crashed through the door. Mum stood there smiling.

"You were quick"

What? She'd disappeared for a week and she was going on about being quick?

"You only left for your friends' a minute ago!"

Jessica looked at the clock. 5.16, July 18. She'd left for her friend at 5.15 on the same day. Jessica had been gone a week but according to the clock she had been gone a minute. Eh?

She went into the living room. The Kosovo report was still on the telly. The picture changed to the refugee camp. The place was burning down as all the people she recognised were running around. She looked at the place she was standing, but she wasn't there! She saw the family she had lived with had survived. Good. Suddenly she knew they would be OK. They were strong.

Mum came through.

"I've been thinking how a mobile 'phone might be useful."

"No, I don't need one. I've got too many luxuries."

Mrs.Smith looked at her daughter strangely.

"What the hell are you trying to say?"

"I think I should give my money to Kosovo instead of blowing it on something I don't need."

"But I thought-"

"I'm very lucky I should share my fortune with those who aren't."

Her mother was confused, but Jessica couldn't explain what had happened. No way would she believe her.

Later that night, Jessica sat down and thought of ways to raise money. Car boot sales, sponsored events etc. She knew that her money wouldn't buy enough necessities for everyone, but every penny counted.

A few days later Jessica watched the news. NATO didn't have to bomb Kosovo any more. We were starting to win. Some agreements were made. Kosovo wasn't entirely peaceful, but it was a big improvement. Kosovans went back home, but returned to nothing but a pile of ash and smoke. It wasn't fair, but it made Jessica even more determined to raise money.

Dragon Fashions

Katie Stanton
(Alfred Barrow)

The dragon is covered in scales.
They change colour.
In the sixties, the fashion was lots of different colours at once,
All changing.
In the seventies, it was circles in squares.
But pinstripes were the only things to be seen in in the eighties.
None of that silly stuff now though.
Now the only thing is the lava lamp effect!

If a dragon fell in love
He would give his sweetheart
A scale from his back
Carved into a love heart
All red and shiny
Saying, "Will you be mine?"

Cats

Cue Cumbria

Stewart Wardlaw (Samuel King's)

The strange way they can fall out of trees,
without a scratch or a graze,
or losing one of their lives

Maybe

Gabrielle O'Connor (St. Joseph's)

What if a war broke out
and to end it we used a
        love potion?
Would we get the soldiers to
drink this potion at tea-time?
Would the armies use it and the
soldiers drop their weapons and
        stop fighting?
How long would it last?
Maybe all the soldiers would
dance round a maypole and
        hug each other.
Maybe they'd go to the seaside,
and run into the sea, bare.
Maybe they'd go to the fair
and eat candy floss and
toffee apples while screaming
        on a ghost train.
Maybe they'd pick up little children
and take them for a tank ride.
Maybe they'd use their gun powder
and explode amazing fireworks into
        the night sky.
And how long would it last?
Maybe only a day,
Maybe forever,
Who knows?

Forty Men or Cannon Fodder

Philip Baxter
(John Ruskin)

Line in line we stand
Like dominoes about to fall
With no choice in our fate
To desert is anarchy, but safe,
To go is to do as our country needs
At a cost,
My boys, thirty-nine young lives
Soon to be ruined
For what?
Who knows?
We go, those at the front falling
Bullet-ridden bodies falling to the floor
Thirty of us left
The boom of cannons, shells fall
Blasts knocking us to the ground
Sending bone to ash in seconds
Twenty of us left
Our knives now drawn
Cutting the barbed wire
Like sitting ducks
We are slaughtered
Ten of us left
Into the trenches
Enemies everywhere
A rain of gunfire
One of us left
Bullets everywhere
Falling to the floor
Vision red as blood
Pain is everything
Blackness
None of us left.

Cue Cumbria

Rainy Day Blues

Jayne Calvert
(Settlebeck)

It's raining, which is no big surprise, for I live in Cumbria! I am incredibly bored..I suppose I could walk the dog, though I'd have to wear a dumb, vile, pink cagool I got for my birthday from Uncle Ron - um - no thanks.

Before, I thought I could watch the telly - anything but *Blue Peter*. Too bad mum was watching *Delia Smith's Guide to Boiling Eggs*.

How about playing loud music and dancing round the room violently, to really annoy the neighbours? No use - they're not in!

I could thrash my sister at Monopoly; let's face it, it's not hard. Pity she's too busy shampooing the cat!

I know, I'll *streak!* Nope, I'll never be able to show my face in public again - or any other part of me for that matter.

I might learn how to knit *Granny's Guide to Woolly Jumpers*. Come to think of it, I'd rather eat my own vomit!

Shall I tease and torment my eight year old brother, saying Man U. football players are all women? No point really, because he supports Liverpool!

I'll moan about the weather and walk round with a face like a slapped bottom. Well, I'm already doing this and...it's *boring!*

Why not - um - do homework? Only as a very, very, last resort.

Oh, I'll just build an ark! Hey, it worked for Noah!

My Granny

Hannah Cleasby (Alfred Barrow)

My granny Gertrude is really funny.
Her favourite food is boiled eggs and honey.
She wears bright colours and flares like a hippy
And travels on a moped that's really quite nippy.
Everyone says my gran's really mad
But I have to say I don't think she's that bad.
At Friday night bingo she acts like a fool
But she makes me laugh, and I think she's dead cool.

Haiku

by Katie Stanton
(Alfred Barrow)

The cat stares blankly
out of the silent window
but nothing happens

My Grandad Bert

Claire Shaw (Alfred Barrow)

We'll Meet Again' is my grandad's favourite song. You see, my grandad Bert still thinks the war is on. He lives in an air raid shelter at the bottom of our garden.

He hasn't been in his own house since he came home from the war when he was twenty-one, because of injuries.

He is now seventy-eight. He still wears his old army uniform and is waiting to be called up to go back to the war.

He only leaves the shelter to collect his pension, which he thinks is the modern-day ration!

The only other time he goes out is on a Wednesday night when he goes to the church hall to sing old war songs at the tea dance.

But the most awful thing is when I bring my friends round and he shouts at them if they are eating sweets.

He tells them Britain is struggling and there are not enough sweets to go round.

How embarrassing!

Cue Cumbria

Siblings

Hannah Shepherd (St Aidan's)

My little brother was the worst thing to hit earth, this side of the nuclear bomb!

I think that while my mum was giving birth to him his brain was squished and it left him permanently damaged. Don't believe me? Listen to this.

By the time he was one, he was drawing graffiti on his cot using crayons and ripping the wallpaper off using his DIY kit!

When he was three we went on holiday with our grandparents to Wales. We were at the top of a vertical hill when my brother released the brake on Grandad's wheelchair....with grandad still in it! Grandad's ankle and pelvis were broken and he was kept in hospital for a week!

On his fourth birthday, my brother took the candles off the cake and threw them at the cat - did I mention they were lit?

On his first day at infant school, he cut off a classmate's pigtails and when he was asked why he did it, he said he thought they would look better stuck to the wall!

He put the class pet, a hamster, into the teacher's biscuit barrel. Mrs Harper had a heart attack and had to be wheeled off in a stretcher!

My brother's now seven and he's stopped being so naughty. In fact his teacher says that he's one of the best in the class!

You might think that everything's OK now....have you met my little sister?

No? You don't know how lucky you are!

The Grass Spoke to Me

Jacki Best &
Polly Smith
(Samuel King's)

Why do you pick my pretty flowers?"
"To bring joy to my house"

"Why do you tread on me?"
"To take a short cut"

"Why do you trim me with that strange machine?"
"So you look neat and tidy"

"Why do you steal the heads off my daisies?"
"I like making chains"

"Why do you play football on me?"
"Because daddy bought me a ball"

"Why are they digging me up?"
"Maybe they're moving you to a better place"

"Why are they putting sticky black stuff on top of me?"
"Maybe to move you easier"

"What have I become?"
"A car park"

The Waterfall

Craig Bell (St.Aidan's)

Water falling from mountains
Flowing violently over cliffs
Smashing off the rocks
Crashing down
To the rapids below.
The loud noise of the waterfall,
Spectacular though deadly
The spray from the falls
Creating a bright rainbow
Small fish being washed away
Through the powerful water
I watch from a distance
Safely.

Bath Time Noises
by Thomas Swannick
(Settlebeck)

Splish, splash, plip, plop
Ploosh, whoosh ,plosh, wash.
Gurgle, gargle, glub, glug
slip, slap,
Burp!

Cue Cumbria

Rivers

Rachel Thomas
(Alfred Barrow)

"The wonderful thing about rivers is, you can never step in the same river twice.
The water's always changing, always flowing"

Summer's here,
the gentle waves are glistening
Deep rock pools shining
The warm waters reflecting your face
The safe meandering water trickling under the bridge...
But on the other side...
Icy cold rapids flooding the land, filled with mud and debris
Roaring waves crashing
Rampant, fast and furious currents
Winter's here

"The wonderful, thing about rivers is, you can never step in the same river twice."

Two Poems

Claire Mattinson (Nelson Thomlinson)

Loch Ness Monster

Och there it is,.
The wee beastie,
With humps and bumps,
In the Mistie,

About a foot long
Do you ken,
Or was it 3 inches
or was it ten?

The triple-humped monster,
In Loch Ness lay
Then the waters rippled,
and it went on its way.

Bananas

Oh what a funny shape
Cracked, bent and lean
They hide in little jackets
of yellow, black and green.

Fear

Martin Gallagher
(John Ruskin)

Fear, stalking in the night
Heart racing
Blood pumping
Legs hurting
Weird calls
Behind me like a strange finger
Pointing
Something hunting
Something coming
Big and frightening
Nothing but darkness
Melting my soul.

Limerick

by Ben Grigg, Matthew Cannon, Michael Bottomley
(Settlebeck)

There once was a Dutch boy called Rudy,
Who went for a swim in the nudie.
He was caught by a lass,
who was fishing for Bass,
and suddenly came over all broody.

Millennium Frogs

Lynsey Galloway (St. Aidan's)

Suddenly the clock struck eleven. Just one hour left of the twentieth century. Would life change completely or would it be just like any other year?

Everyone was very excited, and the closer the next century came, the more excited the world got. Every person was partying, glad to be alive.

The time soon passed. Then ten, nine, eight, seven, six, five, four, three, two, one -

"Hey, look, he's a frog!"

"So is she!"

"And him!"

Why do you think this happened to everyone in the world? Why did everyone turn into frogs?

Because it is a leap year!

Cue Cumbria

Daily Brain Diet

Roderick Allen
(Samuel King's)

Breakfast

A short novel about a cereal killer served with a side plate of exotic equations, a scrabbled egg and a juice riddle to wash it down.

Elevenses

A warm cup of Kenyan quizzes and a couple of crunchy crosswords.

Lunch

A saucy side salad of problems to solve as a starter. A main course of Wilde plays by Shakespeare or Hugo served with a side portion of roast puzzles and a large glass of 18th century French red history. For dessert a hot hangman with an airy anagram and finally a small tray of Turkish Dahlite.

Tea

A cup of Chinese teasers with myths and yoga and a division of pie.

Supper

A bowl of alphabet soup as a starter. For the main course, a fishy enigma (fish is always good for the brain) and a side portion of floppy disks to download (art and algebra is very nice on the disks).

Cue Cumbria

A pint of angles and beerings to drink. For dessert a poem by Mrs Lumpypudding and finally a tray of Tai-cheese.

PS The most important part of the brain diet is sleep.

Thoughts
by Mary-Anne Evison
(John Ruskin)

Everything you do influences time
*
An attention seeker doesn't feel loved
*
Honesty is the first step of improving yourself
*
You can hold something but still not have the grasp of it
*
Two hearts are never one until they have been parted

The Interview

Michael Johnstone (St. Aidan's)

SPORTS REPORTER	So then Biffa Rogers what's your views on your sending off?
BIFFA	I didn't do anything.
S.R	O.K, but the video evidence suggests you hit Matty Saunders in the jaw.
BIFFA	So?
S.R	But surely that's a sending off offence isn't it?
BIFFA	No!
S.R	Right, so you accept that you made physical contact with Saunders but believe the referee was wrong to send you off?
BIFFA	Yes, why do you think I nutted him?
S.R	Yes, we have just received news that the ref is semi-conscious and is nearly talking. But surely after you had punched Saunders and head butted the referee, there was no point in kicking the linesman?
BIFFA	But he called me a name!
S.R	What did he call you?
BIFFA	Erm...Biffa, I think.
S.R	OK Biffa; perhaps shades of the Arsenal game?
BIFFA	Who?
S.R	You know! The game where you ended up brawling with fans and served that four match ban.
BIFFA	Oh yeah! Well lots of players get grief from opposition's fans.
S.R	But they were your fans!

Cue Cumbria

BIFFA   So! Look, are you winding me up?
S.R   No please, put that cosh down! Look, I'm just trying to make sense of that Matty Saunders incident.
BIFFA   Who's he then?
S.R   Oh my God! Back to the studio with Des.

Biffa

Cue Cumbria

Match of the day

**Paul Wren
(Alfred Barrow)**

I am chauffeur-driven to the stadium
(Gran gives me a lift in her mini)

I change into my designer strip
(I put my brother's shorts and stained t-shirt on)

I give my tailor-made lightweight professional boots a final shine
(I rub the mud off my trainers)

The coach gives me a final word of confidence
(The PE Teacher, Dave, tells me to get a move on)

I walk out of the tunnel into the stadium
(I jog nervously onto the windy sports field)

The crowd roars
(Gran cries out,"There's our Jimmy!")

Storm

Patrick Isherwood (John Ruskin)

Craggy mountains loom,
Black, threatening,
A hint of evil,
Brooding like the mighty storm,
That ever tries to destroy
The lone walker,
Crush his indomitable spirit,
Destroy the life that defies nature.

Storm breaks,
Lightning dances,
Illuminating darkness,
A glimpse of brilliance,
Like diamonds,
Flashing across the night sky,
Stabbing down,
A hawk, homing to the kill.

A flash of gold
Illuminates the sky,
Announcing the sun's arrival,
Lighting up the menacing cloud
With scarlet blood brought out
By lightning,
As it stabbed the ground,
Determined to Destroy.

Cue Cumbria

Jesus found in Supermarket Freezer Compartment!

Ben Grigg
(John Ruskin)

The churches are in uproar after finding food types in Dodgefoods supermarket 'mocking' their god. The food includes set meals and Genetically Modified food. The food names range from the oddly named **Jesus Holy Burger, The Last Supper Microwave Dish, Jesus's Roast Dove in Olive Dressing to Holy Grail Wine.**

I went to Dodgefoods store in Dornley and although the food had been taken off the 'shelves', I did see crates of the products. The manager of Dodgefoods, Mr Don Jones, replied to the complaint, saying "Although I've removed the food from my freezers, I feel it probably promotes religion rather than mocks it. After all, more people spend Sundays in the supermarket than in church. It's nice that they can find God in the freezer."

Father O'Brian answered this comment in much distress saying "If this damnation to the Lord isn't banned, then he will strike and bring floods and plague to every host of this product, and those involved will be punished, and their names engraved on the slate of Hell. Those who have consumed this evil will suffer their lives in poverty and famine."

The church are planning to take the producers and company to court. Good luck to the Church! But I have to say the dove is quite delicious.

Escapee

Cue Cumbria

Jenny Kruger
(John Ruskin)

Running, Running, Running, Running, *STOP*.
Hiding, Running, Hiding, Running, *STOP*
Hiding, Crouching Deeply Breathing, *RUN*
Sprinting, Shouting, Cursing, Tripping, *CAUGHT*
Twisting, Turning, Fighting, Scratching, *FREE*.
Thumping, Kicking, Screaming, Biting, *GUN*.
Shooting, Shooting, Yelling, Shooting, *DEAD*.
Crying, Knowing, Guilty, Here goes, *BANG*.
Screaming, Painful, Silence, Stillness, *HELL*.

Cue Cumbria

Not even a Fig Leaf

Beth Robinson
(Nelson Thomlinson)

The pristine baton was poised, bringing the pompous string quartet into a particularly riveting composition of Mozart. However, after some time, the usual clamour of people awaiting an event, drowned the delicate semiquavers to a pianissamo and the clinking of plates from the kitchen defeated the object of the players being there at all.

Everyone was waiting, waiting for the unveiling of this mighty sculpture which was to bring happiness and well-being to a prosperous Millennium. Well that's what the council and the programmes told them.

One of the council members involved with the prestigious project was Margaret Clementine-Jones. A very tall woman with fading 'ash-blonde' hair, rouge on her lips and an infinite amount of nobility flowing around her veins, marched proudly onto the stage, stiffly followed by the chairman of the board who sidled up to the podium, fear prominent on his slightly moist features.

"Ladies, gentlemen, friends of the council. Thank you for joining us today to witness the unveiling of this no doubt beautiful Millennium statue, in honour of Margaret Clementine-Jones." The words sang out of the badly tuned speakers, grating in the ears of the onlookers.

"We must thank our resident artist Mr Roguish, who, with our utmost trust, has been given free reign over the design of our sculpture."
"Being a former member of Grimsby Rugby Club, we are sure he will have contributed a superb piece which will contain the quality and beauty deserved by its model."
"Long may it rest in our community garden to remind us forever of such a pillar of our community, the Honourable Margaret Clementine-Jones."

A dreary round of applause followed, to which Ms. Clementine-Jones raised a regal hand and waved (in a manner not dissimilar to that of the Queen). An elegant smirk evident across her scarlet lips

The time had come, the somnolent crowd picked up slightly as the golden cord was grasped. Regally, the shimmering silk flowed away from around the statue, as the string quartet brought Mozart to a crescendo; almost breaking their taut strings in anguish. the statue was revealed!

A scream tore through the air, a terrible scream. Deadly. This was the only sound across the room as the stunned audience gawped at the statue in the front of them.

Yes, it was Margaret Clementine-Jones, but it was *only* Margaret Clementine-Jones, no shoes, skirt, not even a pearl earring to be seen!.

The event was followed by a distinct thud that rang about the hall as Margaret Clementine-Jones slid elegantly from view.

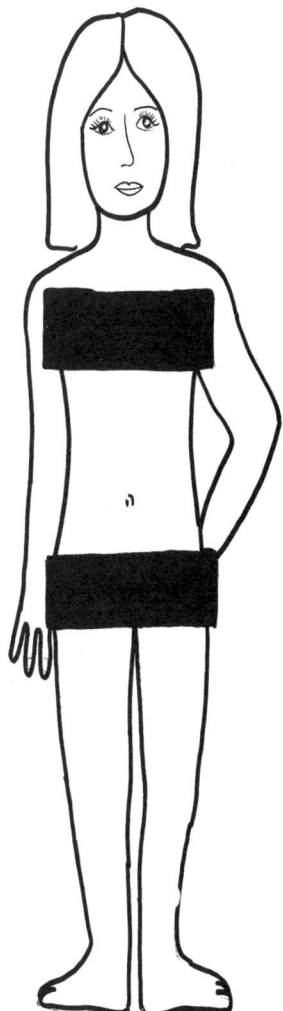

Crisps

Rachel Grennell
(Alfred Barrow)

I would like a packet of crisps,
a packet of tasty, fatty snacks.
How much I love them!

No - I can't eat them,
yet I'm so tempted.
I just simply cannot resist!

I open the packet slowly at first,
Faster and faster,
Then, my hand delves in!

I cram the scrummy crisps into my mouth,
Ooh, they taste so nice.
So nice, that they're all gone!

Cue Cumbria

Excuses! Excuses!

Nick Wright
(Settlebeck)

Monday   " Sorry Miss but I left it at home."
          "Well make sure you bring it tomorrow"

Tuesday   "Sorry Miss but I left it on the bus."
          "I don't believe you Johnny."

Wednesday "What do you mean where's my homework miss? I've already handed it in haven't I?"
          "Don't lie Johnny. I expect it in tomorrow."

Thursday "Sorry miss but - but my sister posted it instead of my granny's get-well card."
          "But you don't have a granny Johnny. Report to me at 1.15."

Friday   "Sorry Miss, but my dad used it as toilet roll 'cos we ran out and and we had curry last night."
          "Johnny I've had enough of this. Take this letter home to your parents."

Scrumptious

Nicola Hall (Alfred Barrow)

I love soft, bouncy, ginger cakes
especially when smothered in custard,
Big, tasty chocolate sponges
piled high in cream,
Airy, flouncy strawberry blancmange
covered with colourful peach segments,
Nice, splishy caramel shortbread
Ooh good enough on its own,
Crumbly, sweet apple lattice
splodged with two lumps of cold ice-cream,
Creamy, sloppy trifle
don't forget the sherry,
Who cares about calories?

Searching

Louise Wilson (St. Aidan's)

In an empty creeky
Ancient house,
I float through walls graciously.
A transparent silky cobweb
As quiet as a locked away secret
Hovering about the floorboards.
I'm as white as snow
As soft as silk
-I'm lonely,
Unhappy, searching for a friend
But as I approach
They only scream a single word
    -GHOST!-

Red

Amy Symonds (Settlebeck)

Red of love,
Red of desire,
Red of the devil,
Burning red fire.

Red hell,
Red night,
Red evil,
Red delight.

Red anger growing,
Red rage created,
Red swirling confusion,
The meaning debated.

Red the rose,
Red of blood,
Small, embarrassed,
Red Riding Hood.

Cue Cumbria

Tortoise

Charlotte Liversidge (Nelson Thomlinson)

I am a one-man army
Slow, consistent, and unstoppable.
Armies learn from my defences,
Writing themselves into the history books.
But I need no army, no followers to send ahead
To be slaughtered in my name.
When danger threatens I need only stop
My victory will be brought about by time.
I have much of that.

Cue Cumbria

Eternal Flame

Ashley Iveson
(Settlebeck)

Billy was thirteen when it happened. That cold Thursday when his mother never returned home. Her flame extinguished in a moment by a crazy kid in a stolen car.

Since that fateful day, Billy had never spoken much. He hadn't only lost his mother but the best friend he ever had.

He would lie awake at night thinking of all the happy times he and his mother shared together. They spent many evenings alone because his father was always working. They had great nights of sharing jokes, watching T.V and listening to their favourite C.Ds. His mum rather influenced his taste in music and he became a great fan of *The Bangles*. They would play the track *Eternal Flame* over and over again. This would be his greatest lasting memory of her.

School had become very difficult for Billy. He never seemed to be able to concentrate on the task in hand, his mind was in other places.

He distanced himself from other children. He was a small vulnerable boy, very much alone in a big cruel world. He became very obstinate and wayward. He pushed the school caretaker off the ladder and let the frogs from the science lab loose in the school! He was crying for attention. His father was no support. Unfortunately, he too was suffering and had thrown himself more into work than ever. The Headmistress was very understanding to begin with and tried to help Billy through this painful period of his life. However, his emotions were a fuel for his anger and the final straw came when he broke into the Headmistress' office and absolutely trashed the place. The Head was absolutely furious and felt she had no alternative but to send him straight home.

He left the school yard ashamed and disgraced. He didn't

know what to do or where to go. He pushed back a strand of brown wispy hair from his tearful face as he wandered down the cobbled street. He didn't want to go back to the cold, lonely house. He slowly wandered past the garden gate and carried on the long lonely road to nowhere.
He passed the village post office and the Bay Tree tea room. He then arrived at the village church and graveyard. All the memories came flooding back. The last time he had been here was to attend his mother's funeral. He approached her grave cautiously. He always thought of graveyards as very spooky places, but now things were different. He knelt down at the graveside and immediately felt a warm sensation. He had an overwhelming feeling of calmness and peace. All his anxiety seemed to disappear in an instant. Suddenly a bright light appeared in front of him, he could see a most beautiful sight. Although it wasn't very clear, he knew at once that it was his mum who had returned to guide him through his problem.

Billy cried with amazement and began to tell her about what had happened at school. He had only just begun when she reached out to hold his hand.
"It's ok Billy, I know exactly what has happened" she said. "You must go and talk to your father- he will understand. I know you don't communicate easily but your father loves you even though he may not show it. He works so hard and feels very alone at the moment. He needs you Billy-you need each other! I must go now "
"No, no," Billy shouted "Don't leave me. "
"Don't be afraid," she said. "I may not always be visible to you, but I will always be watching over you. Think of me as your *Eternal Flame*. I will never disappear from your life altogether. I will be with you in spirit though not in body. My

light will keep burning all around you - never forget that my darling son".

With that she kissed Billy on the cheek and slowly disappeared.

Billy was left alone again, but he was no longer afraid. In fact, he felt a great need to return to his father. He left the cemetry and ran back home. He rushed in and flung his arms around his dad.

"Oh Dad, I've done something terrible."

"Sshh son, don't worry I know everything. Your teacher phoned me this morning and told me all about it. I know it's not like you Billy. I told your teacher that. We've had a good chat-everything's going to be all right."

They held each other closely for the very first time in their lives. Billy put on his favourite track and tears were flooding from his eyes, but not with sadness. They were tears of joy- he now knew his mother had never gone and would never go. She would always be there when Billy felt sad and alone. She would always come and ease his pain. She would never burn out or fade away, she would always be that very special *Eternal Flame*.

Cue Cumbria

Sweet and Sour

Emma Crowe
(Whitehaven)

(My lover's going astray!)

Crowd: Jerry, Jerry, Jerry!
Jerry: Thank you. Today we will be looking at people who are having an affair. Meet Michael
Mike: Hey Jerry.
Jerry: So you're a cheater then?

Mike: Yeah
Jerry: And today you want to reveal the fruity secret to your wife Denise
Mike: That's right Jerry
Jerry: Do you think she'll want a divorce?
Mike: Probably, but I don't want to leave her.
Jerry: So who do you want?
Mike: I want my wife and Sherry, I love them both, I mean my wife is my wife and Sherry is just beautiful. Very tasty! When I look at her I want to eat her, I love her so much, I'm obsessed.
Jerry: We'll see you in a minute, don't go away.
(Commercial Break.)
Jerry: Welcome back, the trauma is really cooking up in here. We've been talking with Michael who is also in love with Sherry who he says is very sweet. Welcome on his wife Denise
(Crowd clap and cheer)
Jerry: Hi Denise
Denise: Hi Jerry
Jerry: So how long have you been married?
Denise: Erm, four years.

Jerry: (*Nodding*) Good relationship?
Denise: Yeah, I love him.
Crowd: Aawww!
Jerry: Well - you want to talk to her go ahead.
Mike: Denise you know I love you.....
Denise: Yeah...but
Mike: But I can't get my lover Sherry out my mind, I can taste Sherry on my lips.
Denise: Oh my God, how could you , you bloody scrub..(*she cries*)
Jerry: Here's Sherry
Crowd: AAAAAGH! (*Shock and disbelief all round*) (*Assistant brings on a sherry trifle*)
Denise: You jelly brained bitch (*she pulls out sherry sponge cake*)
Jerry: Well ladies and gentlemen there we see a troubled man in need of help. So does he choose his wife, or run off with the sherry trifle? See you next time.

Cue Cumbria

Things They Seem To Like Doing

Lynsey Jones (Whitehaven)

Throwing a stick

This seems to exercise their arms greatly. They like to go to parks and open spaces and throw the stick as far as they can. To help them do this, because I am much faster than them, I go and get it for them.

Late night walks

They seem to need exercise just before bed. I always go with them, I have to keep an eye on them, so they don't get lost. I make them wear a lead which they attach to me to just make sure they don't get separated from me. While we are out I make them wait while I see to my toiletry needs and then I take them home.

Throwing balls

They seem to enjoy throwing balls around. They only use a ball when they can't find a stick. The ball goes further than the stick because it bounces so it is easier for them but I have to run a lot further than the balls. They never go and get them, they're always too lazy but I still decide when their ball throwing game ends. As with everything.

Teasing with objects

I have to say I would never have thought anyone could get such pleasure as they do out of teasing me with old shoes and slippers and things. I play along of course; if I didn't I'd upset them and I don't like it when they're in a bad mood.

Teaching obedience

I really do think that my humans are lacking intelligence. They tease and play with things that I rather wish they wouldn't and they complain when I want to teach them obedience. I always let them give the treats out as I get them all, naturally I am the most intelligent amongst our little group. I make them say a word and I do the action it works very well but some times they do it a little wrong. It can't be helped they're only human.

Treats

Their treat-giving service isn't up to my standards. They like giving treats out which I let them do, as any decent dog would. They don't get some of the things I tell them to do, I often say "woof", which any other human would understand as 'GET THE TREATS OUT' but they look at me as if I'm stupid. It can't be helped, because as I've said they're only human.

The Unicorn

Clare Stewart (St. Aidan's)

Cue Cumbria

I can run for miles

galloping wild and free,

throwing my head up in the sky

I carry my horn with pride.

My beautiful tail & mane blown away by the thrashing wind

my body as white as snow falling from the moonlit sky

My golden hooves strike upon the ground like grinding metal

my eyes are fireworks sparkling bright,

if you saw me, my image would splinter your heart.

But why can't you see m?, It's a terrible shame,

I am cast into make-believe,

merely an imaginary animal in a mythical play

Cue Cumbria

Betrayal
(extract)

John O'Connor (Nelson Thomlinson)

The council sat in the vast stone hall that was the nucleus of the Borach underground city. Ornate tapestries hung from the walls depicting titanic battles from the Borach history and famous stories of legend.

The Borach king sat on his impressive throne. He was dressed in fine robes, which were stained with remains from the feast. A ginger beard flowed over his stomach down to his knees. His bushy eyebrows seemed as thick as his hair. Around him sat other members of the council who were relaxing after a good meal, joking and merrymaking.

Suddenly the hall doors swung open and stale air wafted over the Borach lords. A messenger named Snikket who was quite tall and stout strode into the great hall. "Sire", he said in an anxious tone, deep lines carved into his forehead from stress. "I bring grave news".

"Well boy don't just stand there, spit it out." As the king spoke beer spluttered from his mouth over the remains of his meal.

The messenger looked at the king in disgust. "Sire, the miners will not be able to glean any more wealth from the pitiful old seam. We must find new gold to mine if we are to continue buying our supplies instead of making them ourselves. The closest and by far the richest lies in Sylvian teritory. I strongly suggest that we expand our borders and take it from them.

"Declare war on them! Snikket you snivelling worm you would attack those who befriended and helped us?" roared the king. His cheeks glowed hot as red coals.

Snikket scowled inwardly at the vile toad. He had less idea about governing a kingdom than a sewer rat. Whilst the pompous ass was stuffing himself with exquisite food and fine ales his people would be starving because of his gross incompetence. "Perhaps I might negotiate a deal" said Snikket in a voice that masked his hatred for the king.

"Very well" the king grumbled. "Anything to get you out of my sight!"

Lightning
by Amy Lawrence
(Whitehaven)

I had an argument with thunder last night,
It turned into a really nasty fight,
He reckoned he was better than me,
"I'm number one, just wait and see!"
First I brought light to the dark night sky,
"There," I said," now you have a try!"
The enemy thunder vibrated the blanket of blue.
"Now," he says," let's see if you can match that too!"
Now, I fulfilled my life long-desire,
I struck down vital electricity wires.
Thunder made poor children wail,
But he didn't care(typical of a flaming male).
Next I went for Whitehaven Candlestick,
Perhaps another barbecued tree would do the trick,
I went to prove lightning strikes the same place twice
for I didn't strike once , twice but THRICE!
Thunder stood by, pretty cheesed off,
He knew only too well that he had lost,
"Okay," he says."You won fair and square,
but I think we could work well as a pair.
So next time we want to make everyone scream,
what about doing it as a team?"

Some water talk............ (St.Joseph's)

Kimberley Swinburne (St. Joseph's)

the Parti!
Bi Jordans

Tooday I went too Beth 6 Birfday Parti at her howse She liced her prezent we played gams and I had som jeli and sosij roles I cudeled the hamster chuci and I gived it a baf in the toylet and I puled the handel the hamster was gon beths dady was lowd and angri but I dident cri.

The driving lesson from hell

Gavin Routledge
(St. Aidan's)

She got into the driving seat
Dad got in as well
He fastened up his seat belt
He knew this would be hell.

She started up the engine
With a big almighty roar
Put her hands upon the steering wheel
And her foot down to the floor.

They shot out of the driveway
Like a rocket into space
She looked across at dad
And saw the horror on his face.

She skimmed close by a man
Who was pedalling his bike
He swerved, skidded and wobbled
As he fell into the dyke.

The traffic light turned red
She just went straight through
Dad began to cry
The air was turning blue.

Half an hour later
They shot back up the drive
Dad was in a state of shock
Though glad to be alive.

A Life is so Important

Roxanne Kliszat (Settlebeck)

A life is so important
I saw my sister's life go like lightning.
So calm and brave.
Seeing her face disappearing
through the glass
when the ambulance doors closed.
The bad news a day later
"Mum where's heaven?" I asked.
"She's gone to watch us from above
To see you get old," said mum.
"One day you'll see her again."
Till then I miss her.

NB: This poem was written about Roxanne's sister, Rowena who died.

Tiger

Cue Cumbria

Stefenie Anderson (Nelson Thomlinson)

My mercury flesh ripples,
Gliding over powerful bones.
I stroll a sultry swagger
Across to tough weathered earth.
My torso a mass of ball bearings
Surrounded by a velvet cloak.

   Attacked by sun;
   blinded I kill.

My fur is my fame;
my flaw, my downfall.
Hunters' eyes narrow,
Prepare trigger and sights while I model
Next season's fashion
To a bullet's fatal applause.

A design for the cat-walks of an ignorant world.

Cue Cumbria

The Baby Vampire
(opening extract)

Rachel McAlone
(Whitehaven)

Outside the sun rose to reveal a beautiful December day. It was eight o'clock and the shadows on the ground were fifty metres long. Everywhere the creatures of the night fled the coming dawn. Foxes to their earths. Owls to their roosts. Bats to their cave, attics, belfries. Badgers to their setts. Vampires to their crypts.

The creatures of the day stretched and climbed up to greet the sun. Birds sang, and fluttered about. People left for school, work and the outside world. Cows wandered their frosty fields contentedly. All was well in the mortal world.

The day pssed as all do. The sun floated from east to west. Children laughed and played. Adults wandered the streets and typed their letters. Rabbits hopped around in the cool air. Deer pranced around the forests. Otters played and swam in rivers.

Eventually the sun sank; rabbits witnessed this without much worry, they were at home in the dark more than the day. Birds flocked for perches. Many humans rushed for home. Tough teenagers stayed out after moonrise. Badgers emerged from their sets sniffing the twilight air. Foxes left their earths leisurely trotting into the dark. Bats left their caves and squeaking, greeted the night. In other places vampire eyes snapped open.

Quinn stuck his tongue out. He was desperately thirsty. He crawled out of his sickeningly bright coffin and wandered out the door. In his old home his mum's room was just down the corridor. In this house the stairs were there. Quinn didn't know that - at least before he fell down them.

Quinn burst into tears "Mummy!"

"Mummy's here!" The vampire picked the boy up and hugged him.

Quinn remembered his mum, he loved her. He stopped crying and stuck his thumb in his mouth. Then Quinn remembered last night.

"Aagh!" Quinn began to cry twice as much as before. "Put me down, put me down!"

"Okay!" She put him down and backed away. Quinn ran down the hallway.

"Quinn come back!" Mrs Wight called after him. "George".

Quinn ran through the door into a coldly lit steet. There were three or four kids on the street corner. He loped past them hoping the vampires wouldn't follow him.

"Hey you're that white boy." a tall boy from the group called. "Ain't ya?"

"Can't talk. Vampires after me." Quinn replied without stopping.

"Vampires?" a short boy from the group called.

"Yeah."

"Aren't you a vampire too?" A girl asked.

"No."

"I am," the girl said sweetly.

Recipe for a Perfect Day of Trouble

Gemma Staunton
(Alfred Barrow)

Ingredients
An annoying mother
A straight face
An innocent voice
A believable story

Recipe

Take one heated up mother and one daughter chilled. Put them together and add harsh words. Make sure the daughter has a nicely rolled out straight face.

Meanwhile bring the mother to the boil and remove when steaming.

Whilst hot mix in a couple of arguments and using a sieve, separate mother from daughter and allow to settle.

Put in fridge to cool and reheat tomorrow for another perfect day of trouble.

Cue Cumbria

Ivan Idea

Hannah Robinson (Nelson Thomlinson)

A round the year 1850 a child came into the world who was to become, in later years, Wigton's most famous son after he founded its most notorious feature - the metallic frame we now refer to as UCB Films.

As the child aged into adulthood, he grew arachnid limbs and gnarled digits. His head balded unusually early and he developed an unhealthy obsession with shoelaces. There could only be one vocation for him; it was only a matter of time before he accepted his fate and became a librarian.

His name, you ask? The rather apt Ivan Idea (much better than his birth name of John Smith).

After a number of years however, the novelty of dictating angry telegrams to overdue borrowers had worn off and Ivan decided to fulfil a lifelong ambition and open a factory. However, the only plot of land available was beside Wigton's first (and rather putrid) cesspit.

Despite this, Ivan carried out his plans and the plastic-making factory thrived - there was only one problem. The inhabitants of Wigton were becoming very unhappy. Eventually after an urgent meeting of the townspeople, the Wigtonians decided to banish Ivan due to the horrific smell and the unsightly 'lish-losh' colour of the local river caused by the factory.

Disgraced, Ivan retreated to the small village of Snooton where he designed the stylish council block architecture that we are still familiar with today. This concept was applied to Snooton which, after years of construction, eventually grew into the concrete paradise of Birmingham, where Ivan later died aged ninety-nine and three-quarters.

Lost and Found

Caroline Haigh (Settlebeck)

Lost

I have lost my homework

It's really really good

It's a home EC essay

on how to make a pud

My name's Sarah Wing

I'll do anything

to get my treasured piece of

homework back.

P.S. Hurry up it's due in on Tuesday!

Found

I found a piece of homework
which is just a dreadful fright

It's on about a pudding!

I found it last night

Come and pick it up

before I put it in the bin.
But to hand it to the

teachers would be a real sin.

Mrs. White
27 Moorway road
Stafford

The life of a Lift

Laura Robson
(Samuel King's)

I'm not any old lift
I can see everything that goes on inside of me,
Those secret affairs and yes, you picking your nose.

The old woman who talks to herself,
The four girls who start dancing to the music,
And the young boy who kicks his football against the side of the lift.

The secretary who puts her make-up on before going to work
The business men talking about new developments
Then you get the people who spit in me and use me as a rubbish bin.

So when you climb inside me
Remember I'm watching
So don't make me mad and I won't break down

Cue Cumbria

Santa's Letter

Thomas Prince
(St. Aidan's)

Santa's Little Cottag
Old Fort Lock
PA3 1LT
Greenland

Dear Peter,
    Thank you for writing. Hope you are being good in your big mansion. I understand that you want these things:

BMW 23 - You're a bit too young to drive.
Combat shotgun - Your parents won't be too pleased.
Loch Ness Monster - I don't think it will fit in your swimming pool.
Manchester United Football Club - Even you can't afford £600,000,000
for the richest club in the world.
Cartoon Network - Haven't you already got the channel on Sky digital?
World Domination - I don't think anyone wants an eight year old boy running the planet.
5,000 Army troops - Sorry.
2,000 Tanks - Oh my God!
200 Submarines - Are you on some sort of medication?

Maybe you should give Mrs. Claus a ring on 01880MERRY XMAS. She is a child psychiatrist and she can probably help you. Okay, see you December 25th, goodbye.
               Yours sincerely,
               Santa Claus

Cue Cumbria

Beginnings

Toby Hine
(John Ruskin)

It is hard to write of the time before I came to this place. In those days I was not rooted in space, nor even firmly embedded in time. You could say that I drifted and listened to the sound of the stars singing.

There was beauty there - in the shimmering glories of star clusters, burning gems in dark velvet space, fiery tongues of incandescence roaring from the boiling suns, the delicate peppering of dust and gas, mountains of ice tumbling through the darkness, the sudden inky black of dark nebulae and the terrorising vortex of pulsing neutron stars.

I saw both the great and the small-frenzied popping and sparking in the space between atoms and the slow twists and curls of whirlpool galaxies. And not merely colours - so many senses beyond the simple material-the sweet jasmine scent of comet's tail, the heady taste of iron in the hot core of the stars, the thousand whispers of a dying supernova, the delicate caress of hydrogen streamers, and a million impressions besides......

How long did I ride the solar winds? I have no measure. In those days there was only I, an amorphous cloud of consciousness without language or yardstick, washed on the eddies of time. A long while I suppose. But in the end, I came to the radiance of Earth.

I was drawn to it, like a salmon to the ghostly taste of his home river or a moth fluttering closer to a fatal candle flame. In the darkness in front of me; Earth. It glowed. It shone. The rush of energy streaming into space dizzied me. It was intoxicating. Startling.

Roaring power flowing like a river, and yet somehow, not quite tangible. It tortured me, that torrent that was so close to being a part of me and yet so subtly alien that I could not quite fathom how to dip my fingers into its glittering flow. Almost I left Earth. I must anchor myself in that matter and sacrifice the freedom to roam the stars.

It was with earthly senses that I felt the stones beneath me begin to tremble as I reached deep into the rock and began to pull. There was a grumbling roar as pinnacles and spires of stone stabbed upward into the sky. Walls and towers of gleaming, polished marble, intricate minarets and turrets. It was my first sculpture-and though the medium was crude and cold, I took pleasure in the strength and beauty of my citadel. It was my focus. And yet....even anchored as I was, in the earth and dust of the planet, still its power evaded me. Still it gushed and flowed and hurtled about me and still I could not grasp it. Angry now I tried to hurl the clouds against one another and stir the air into a boiling hurricane - and there was nothing. Not only was the beautiful song of the stars denied to me now, but even the most basic of my powers had gone. I knew pain and sorrow. The shining towers of my citadel mocked me as my strength faded. I could no longer see into the spaces between atoms. I was blind to the stars, and deaf to their song. I was shrinking, dimming, a light almost snuffed out. Soon there would have been nothing left but the faintest shadow of a sad ghost, whining on the wind, and dreaming of what once was...

And then... a creature. A tiny fleshy little insect crawling to the walls of my tower. A human - its skin pale, wet with the rain, shivering in the cold wind, its hair plastered to its head, a little insignificant speck. And yet within it...something. A seed; a tiny spark of fire. Curious, I swept closer. It knelt before the curtain of rock surrounding my prison, and raised its arms high, and then- ahhhh! A sudden, delicious, glorious sweetness! Power! Power like a drug, an ecstasy of power! Pleasure so intense it was almost pain. This tiny, puny, half-naked animal held the key to the whole power of Earth! As it knelt and worshipped I felt myself increase and begin to shine again. I looked beyond the little flicker of consciousness of the man who knelt at my gates, and sensed others. They were the source of the radiance, the fatal glow that had drawn me here! It was not the world, but the little creatures crawling on its surface! There were dozens of them. Hundreds. The thought of that giddy surge of power multiplied five hundred-fold made me tremble and shudder with longing.

And I knew then what I had to do. The people of Earth, and their whole world, must be mine.

Short Poem
by Hannah Shepherd
(St Aidan's)

Imagine if the world was square
and all the trees were round,
if all the birds forgot their wings
and never left the ground.

Experimental

Amy Wakefield (Alfred Barrow)

"I think she's the ideal candidate for our experiment," said the Chief Master staring down through his powerful Cobble Wogger.

Kim, who had no idea she was being watched, dragged herself slowly towards her school.

"No," said the Master's wife, "that's a pig! I'm not having my son touching something like that. I want a proper specimen for him to experiment on."

"We haven't got time," said the Master, beaming his son to earth.

The Chief Master's son was the best looking Cobblewog in the whole galaxy. He had a brilliant figure. He was medium-sized with blue-brown hair and two blue tufts at each side of his head. His mouth was yellow with great big bulgy luscious lips and his nose was very small - almost pointy at the end. His arms and legs were very stumpy though and that was his downpoint because when he walked his arms wiggled and he waddled like a penguin. One thing about him that no-one could understand was that he had white feet.

Kim was walking back from school. She'd had an awful day and she was slowly crawling home, dragging her bag behind her. Then she looked up and saw two white feet. She looked up a little more and couldn't believe her eyes. All that came out was a large scream.

Cue Cumbria

Bothersome Sister

Toni Gilmore
(St.Joseph's)

<u>10 ways to deal with a bothersome sister</u>

1   Put her in a washer, hang her out to dry and iron her with a tray.

2   Freeze her in an ice cube.

3   Tie string to her fingers and sell her as a kite.

4   Turn her upside down to mop up the kitchen.

5   Put her in the mixer, shove her in the oven, sit her on a plate and serve her up like chocolate.

6   Tie her up with bubble gum.

7   Squash her into a golf ball, try for a hole in one.

8   Strap her to a rocket and send her to the moon.

9   Plant her in compost, water her every day and grow her into a bonsai tree.

10 Lock her in a small dark cupboard.

Cue Cumbria

When I walk Down the Street

Tom Swannick (Settlebeck)

When I walk down the street I see
lots of different people, none like me.

I go into the newsagents to buy a bag of sweets,
Cor! Shut up! That guy over there must think he's Elvis
He sounds terrible (what a dramatist).

I reach the counter. "Hello, hello, erm, excuse me?"
Stupid woman hasn't noticed me.
She's busy talking to herself (stupid fool).

As I leave the newsagents a bunch of lads;
Spitting, swearing, shouting
(Rebellious teenagers).

Stealthily avoiding the mob - a wooden bench:
upon it, two characters, holding hands, petting
and then up a gear into a full snog. Ugh!
(Love-sick adolescents).

Long queue in the post-office
Please! This guy in front of me is picking his nose very obviously
And I'm sure that he's just farted
(Dirty creep).

The journey home, a humble stroll
Zzzoom! Hey, watch it!
Two kamikaze kids just crossed my path at a frightful pace
(Stupid kids).

Now I am home and all the things I see
I realise that any one of those guys could be me.

Cue Cumbria

Life is a River
(A Soliloquy)

Mary-Anne Evison
(John Ruskin)

A river is life, always flowing, always changing. We have to adapt to these changes. The connected streams that unite into one river are the paths we choose in life - paths leading to success, paths leading to fortune, paths leading to happiness. The river is free, we have freedom of choice. The tributaries, which together converge to form a river, represent growth. Waterfalls cascade with the exuberance of youth.

The journey through the rapids shows that life consists of ups and downs. The stones on the riverbed represent the hard bits of life we pass along the way.

But remember a river's always flowing - we have to keep going! The rate of flow of a river is the greatest near its source. The river starts off narrow and fast, signifying birth and development. It widens towards the end, showing our achievements, greater knowledge of life, what we've obtained from life. It ends much slower, signifying old age, meandering on its way, portraying an elderly person rambling on.

Approaching its mouth it usually passes through a broad flood plain consisting of sedimentary material that the river itself has deposited. We are giving back some of the knowledge and experience gained.

Eventually our life ends.

However, the river is continuous and never stops. Evaporation represents our gradual passing-on. Life is given back to the river in the form of rain. This all forms *The Circle of Life*.

The Over-Enthusiastic Dad

Louise Bell (St. Aidans)

"Get a hobby!" Mum said to Dad. Big mistake! Dad chose photography. Now he never leaves home without his beloved camera. He takes it to parties, weddings, outings, holidays. You name the occasion, and dad has his camera.

He is driving us nuts!

I mess around in my bedroom, singing into my hairbrush, Dad comes in and *SNAP!* - he has me on film.

"They've come out lovely," Mum says, with great doubt in her voice.

"Get a life Dad! Please, before we all go crazy Dad! Get a new hobby Dad!"

I've tried jigsaws, but when Dad had finished making them he just took photos of them. I tried a Playstation with ten different games, but dad just kept pausing the screen and taking pictures. Then he sent the pictures off to the Playstation magazine with a review attached. I tried books, but he just wasn't interested.
So I hired a therapist, but it didn't work!

Mum tried a new strategy.
"If you don't give up photography, then I will take the kids and live at my mother's house till you do!"
Well, it worked! Only now, dad is into video cameras. This is not the way my life should be!

Cue Cumbria

Mismatch -
(A Short Play)

Aimee Henry
(Whitehaven)

(David and Lynsey are on the aeroplane)
DAVID: How much longer do we have to sit on this plane?
LYNSEY: Not much longer
DAVID: I can't feel my legs, I'm bored stiff and in case you hadn't noticed, I wish I was at home
LYNSEY: Oh shut up David, we'll be there in two hours
DAVID:. Two more hours cooped up on this thing! I'll have starved to death by then!
LYNSEY: You and your stomach! Just think, in two hours' time, I'll be sitting by the pool in the hotel, sunning myself in the gorgeous Florida heat
DAVID: I won't. I'll be finding a TV showing English football
LYNSEY: Typical!
DAVID: Well, I want to watch the FA Cup Final. I just hope we'll make it in time. *(He shoves his headphones on and switches the radio on. He falls asleep)*
******
LYNSEY: Wake up David!
DAVID: Um - what?
LYNSEY: We're just about to land *(He sits up straight, and adjusts seatbelt)*
DAVID: Thank God! What time is it?
LYNSEY: It's half-past ten
DAVID:. Half-past ten? You're having a joke aren't you?
LYNSEY: No, look *(She shows him her watch)*
DAVID: We were supposed to land at at half-past nine

Cue Cumbria

LYNSEY: It takes nine hours to get there, not eight
DAVID: Oh God, I'm going to miss it! We've got two
DAVID: hours to kick-off. *(The plane lands and passengers get off)*

******

DAVID:. It's true what they say, you know
LYNSEY: What are you babbling about?
DAVID: More hurry, less speed. We'll have to get through the customs really quickly, then grab our luggage and run.
LYNSEY: Forget it. If we try to do it, we'll ruin the start of our holiday. *(David mutters under his breath)*
DAVID: Just wait and see *(He grabs hold of Lynsey's arm and he drags her with him)*
LYNSEY: David, what are you playing at? *(Bumping into people).* I'm sorry madam. David. Stop it. Excuse us!
DAVID: See, we're at the front of the queue now and we did no-one any harm
LYNSEY: We were so rude though
DAVID: Nobody noticed us. Come on, keep walking. *(They approach the customs)*
AIRPORT OFFICIAL: Passports please! *(Asks a series of questions).* OK, thank you, enjoy your vacation
LYNSEY: I'm sure we will *(They go to wait for luggage)*
DAVID: How many more green bags can there be?
LYNSEY: Just wait - there can't be many left now. There! Quick - grab them!

DAVID: Let's go! *(They leave the airport)* Taxi!
DRIVER: Where you guys going?
LYNSEY: The Floridian International Drive please
DRIVER: Righto then *(Takes them to the hotel)*
LYNSEY: This isn't what the hotel in the brochure looked like!
DRIVER: Well, you said the Floridian Suite
DAVID: No, she just said the Floridian!
DRIVER:. It's all the same to me
DAVID: You'd better get us to our hotel, right now! I've got an important Cup Final to watch in less than one hour and if I miss it there'll be trouble. *(The taxi speeds to the hotel)*
LYNSEY: This is the right one, thanks
DAVID: And we'll only be paying half the money *(The taxi driver accepts this. They pay. David goes into the bar, looking for a TV)*
BARMAN: Hi - how can I help you?
DAVID: By telling me you've got a TV broadcasting English football
BARMAN: Ah yes. The FA Cup. Yes, we do have a TV. Do you want to know the score?
DAVID: What do you mean? It hasn't kicked off yet. It's only a quarter to twelve.
BARMAN: Bad news sir. You're four hours late. You forgot to turn your watch back. Liverpool won one nil.
DAVID: I don't believe it, I missed it. This holiday was destined to be a nightmare. I just knew it!

(End of play)

Cue Cumbria

Granny's Shopping List

Elizabeth Fye (Workington)

Chemist
Hair dye - beach babe blonde
Perfume - Tommy Girl
Lipstick - Purple Plum
Teeth bleaching kit - Bright White
Nail varnish - Scarlet delight
N.B (Go to vet and ask for muzzle for Killer)

Supermarket
Champagne - for date on Sunday

Clothes
For the rave - Sequinned boob tube - purple
Knee boots - silver?
Mini skirt - black
Devil horns headband - for Killer
Black leopard-skin pants - maybe?
N.B (Hire hall and D.J. for rave)

Bits and bobs
Trance tape - for Saturday's date
Pleated skirt, cardigan, slippers, tights
N.B (remember thick ones),
blouse and wig - for Sunday when the family come.
N.B (Ask Pete to come and take disco ball down)

Remember
To pick up new motorbike helmet.

Cue Cumbria

Tornado Tim

Alexander Stewart (Workington)

Tornado Tim's got a problem,
It's all to do with his nose.
It seems to keep on exploding,
And causing torna-dose.

ATCHOO!

The wind is worse than a gale,
It comes with cat, dog and hail.
The sky turns black , TT sneezes,
And the tornado starts again.

ATCHOOO!

When he sneezes there's mayhem all round.
Trees are uprooted like twigs,
Slates fly off like hats,
Ladies dresses are lifted with ease.

ATCHOOOO!

Dr Custard has tried to fix it, but it's all been in vain.
He's used every lotion and potion,
But TT always sneezes again.

ATCHOOOOO!

A leap year, 2000 today,
This sneeze will be the biggest yet.
He's filled up with air and all sorts,
He's blowing..... it's gonna come out,

ATCHOO!
ATCHOOO!!
ATCHOOOO!!!

R.I.P (maybe)

Cue Cumbria

Imogen McGarvie (Samuel King's)

(Please lie on your side to read this page)

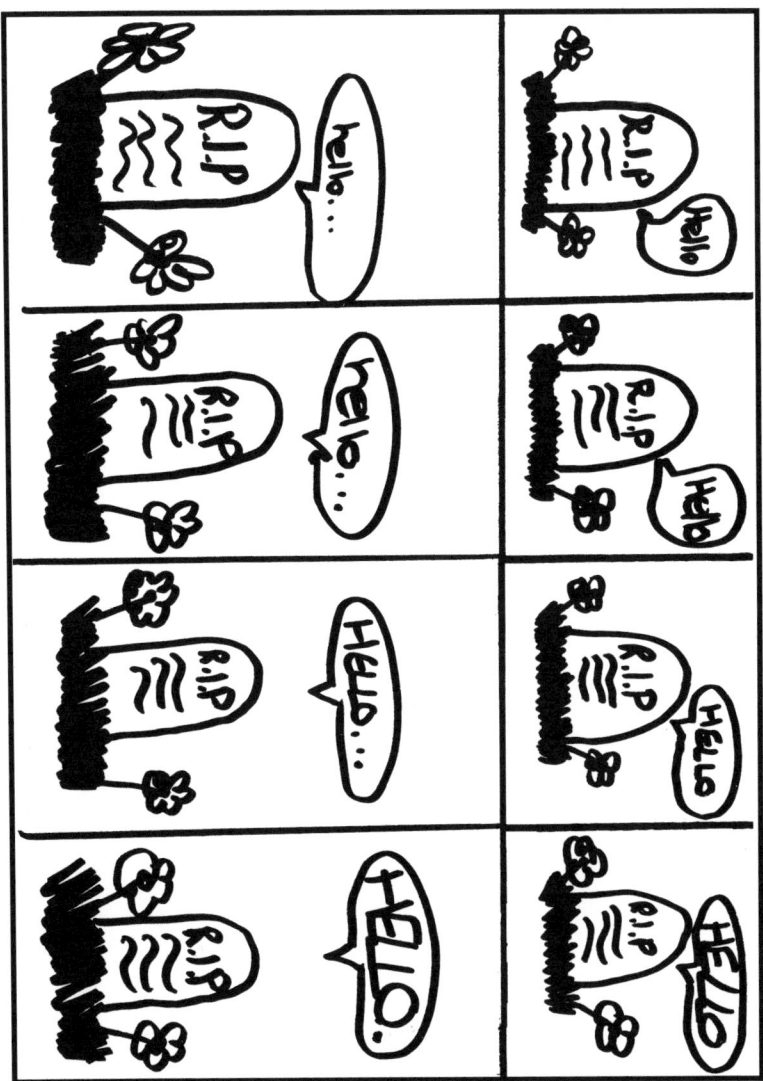

Two Poems

Tom Smith
(John Ruskin)

Adrenalin Rush

It pushes adrenalin through the body.
The effect of flying takes control
as your body is left in a trance
while the mind is freed
Freed into the world where anything happens,
Images of darkness, the infinity of space.
The boundless, harsh environment of the mind.

*Written whilst listening to Mars, God of War,
by Gustav Holst*

Black Illusion

Black is evil, it possesses the night,
The Colourless vision's blind to sight,
Black is an endless vacuum of Limbo and Death,
The infinite scream of a silent breath,
But black is empty and emptiness is nothing,
But nothing is not there,
So black is an illusion,
Only in your mind.

Cue Cumbria

Fish Wish

Martyn Metcalfe
(St. Joseph's)

Steven was always on the run from his parents after they'd shouted at him for being so untidy. His room was a mess, so was his life and he lied through his front teeth day or night. One day he retreated to the beach at Workington to get away from his parents' nagging. Along the beach he strolled, muttering and spluttering, throwing pebbles into the water, when suddenly a pebble was thrown back at him from out of the sea.

He threw back a rock and a large hand with a fish in its grasp slapped him silly. A dark figure rose out of the sea. "What's this?" exclaimed Steven "Am I in a movie set? Are you an extra from a sea monster movie from Mars? Are you a drunk from a fancy dress party?"

"No I am from Subaquavil and I am really hungry."

"What's Subaquavil, dork?"

"It's a secret camouflaged city under the sea, you little brat."

"And why are you angry, dipstick?"

"For years your race has been polluting my home, and now we are going to obliterate you, banana head."

"No you're not."

"Yes, we are."

"No, you're not."

"Are."

"Not."

"Are."

"Not."

"Are, are."

"Not, not."

"Are, are, are, barzy, jinx, full stop, not return."

"Not, fish breath."
"Oh go and tell your people we are coming, pea brain."
Steven ran back to his home and blurted to his parents: "There's an army coming from Subaquavil to destroy us."
"Oh no Frank, he's been at the glue again. Now Steven you're going to be O.K. Come and lie down."
"No, no we have to call Scotland Yard, the Army, MI5"
"He's had more than I thought."
They huddled Steven into his room and locked the door.
"Oh great, The Bill's coming on T.V"

Meanwhile the Subaquavil had traced Steven to his home. He walked up to the door. "How do I get in? There's no transporter. Maybe this button will work"
Inside the bell rang frantically.
"Frank answer that, I'm watching The Bill."
"Well so am I, answer the door."
"No you answer it."
"Oh bugger this." The Subaquavil smashed through the wall.
"Frank, you answer it."
"No, you answer it."
The Subaquavil cleared his throat."I am here to avenge your pollution to my world. I said I am here to avenge for my

people for all the times you have polluted the rivers, the seas and the oceans."
"Salted the liver, the peas and the lotion? Are you alright love?"
"Yes I said............."
"Hang on love, a solvent smeller is about to get arrested. Go on son, give em some stick."
"I am here to turn you into a fish," proclaimed the Subaquavil.
"Hush love, I can't hear the TV. Go and make yourself a cuppa."
"Alacazam." The Subaquavil turned the parents into fish. They continued to watch T.V as if nothing had ever happened.
"Oh it's you fish breath."
"I've turned your parents into fish."
"Oh brilliant."
"And now you're next."
"What? You don't want to turn me into a fish."
"Why not?"
"Listen, I'll stop calling you fish breath if you don't turn me into a fish."
"O.K but the first time I hear you call me fish breath, you'll be one yourself."
"It's a deal, where we going now?"
"What's your capital?"
"Oh that's London."
"Who's an important figure in London?"
"Why, that's the Queen."
"O.K, we go to London and turn the Queen into a fish."
"O wicked!"

Cue Cumbria

Generation
(A play: opening extract)

Natalie Craig
(Whitehaven)

Mam You're not seeing him and that's final.
Jess I can do as I please.
Mam No you can't, if you're living under this roof.
Jess Well I'll move out.
Mam No you won't. You're only fourteen.
Jess Jake says I'm old enough to move out and do as I please.
Mam Well I'm not Jake.
Jess Thank God for that.
Mam For once in your life listen to what your mother has to say.
Jess Why should I ? You only give crap advice anyway
Mam Well you have to listen to someone when you're going out with a lad like him. I mean how would you cope? He wouldn't know what to do because he lives in that run-down area with all that lot.
Jess Which lot?
Mam All those on that estate.
Jess What's wrong with the estate?
Mam Well for starters, there are no full panes of glass in the windows, the garden looks like a jungle, all the cars are burnt-out and parked on the curbs, not in the garage. Need I go on?
Jess You usually do.
Mam Stop being so damn cheeky.
Jess What would you know at your age?
Mam Well I've dealt with this kind of behaviour before.
Jess What with dad? You really held onto him, didn't you?
Mam We had a steady relationship going for ten years as a matter of fact.

Cue Cumbria

Jess Steady - is that what you call it? Sleeping with about ten different men.
Mam No I never, anyway where did you hear that?
Jess Dad.
Mam He's a liar.
Jess Don't you call my dad a liar. You're the liar. It was you who broke the marriage off. It's your fault. Everything's your fault. I hate you. I really do hate you.
Mam You don't know what you're saying.

Jess I do know what I'm saying. I hate you.
Mam No you don't. Now go to your room and calm down. You should think about what you've just said to me. I'll be waiting down here for an apology.
Jess You're not getting an apology from me. You should give me one.
Mam No I shouldn't. Now go to your room.
Jess No.
Mam Now!
Jess I hate you.

Cue Cumbria

What a day

Paula Price
(Alfred Barrow)

Oh no, it's nine,
I'm late, I'm late, I'm late
For the wedding.
Must hurry
Change outfit
Not so good,
what the heck!
Drop keys down drain
Get them out
What a smell!
Car won't start
Phone taxi
Guess who's here?
My taxi
Driven by my ex
Wanting to talk
"No time"
I scream
"Just drive!"
Arrive all wet
Look for family
Forget that!
Bride march starts
Oh no! Wrong church
Wrong time
Wrong bride.

Cue Cumbria

Untitled

Beth Dodd
(John Ruskin)

Birth

Warmth and protection surround
A blissful serenity
Uncomplicated mind-
Sleeping in a cocoon of tranquility
Alive

A tunnel opens up
For the first-time light
Reach towards the light
Sound, smell, sight,
Explore new awareness

Death

Voices drift away into murmurs
Soothing accompaniment to a flickering heartbeat
The lights are fading
At peace

A tunnel opens up
For the first time, true light
Reach towards the light.....

Cue Cumbria

Home sweet home

Jessica Thompson (Settlebeck)

Walking up the stoney path,
Towards my loving home,
I open the door,
And try to ignore
My mother's echoing screaming
My brother's pathetic teasing
Granny sitting in her old wooden chair,
mumbling to herself.
My father's terrible DIY work,
Books tumbling off the shelf.
I carry on my dangerous journey,
up the stairs to my room,
But find to my horror,
my diary, left strewn,
Half of it missing.
Down stairs I head, towards my dog's bed
Where I find my lost secrets.
Rescuing them, I sit and read alone,
About all the family,
And how I moan.
I look around and all I see,
Is all my family, and, of course me.

I love them really.

The Lost Painting
(A ghost story - extract)

**Caroline Eden
(Whitehaven)**

Utterly dejected, I walked back down the corridor. A line of portraits caught my eye. As I drew closer, I realised they were all of Francis, of when he was a baby, to the age he was now. There were about twenty portraits in all. A kind of visual timeline, I suppose.

I noticed that there was a portrait missing - just a bare space on the wall, a gaping hole where it should have been. I guessed from its position in the line and the portraits around it, Francis should have been around eighteen when it was painted. Not thinking anything of it, I walked out of the manor down the road and up to the river.

I sat on the bank on a large rock, propped my head on my hands and thought. Why wouldn't Margaret tell me how Mary had died? The rhythmic sloshing of the water took up residence in my brain. Droplets of water glistened when the afternoon sun caught them. I couldn't think. I shook my head. Stared blankly at the river, rolling down to the sea. A reminder of something......something.

Suddenly it clicked. I remembered. Three squiggles Mary had drawn under her name in the diary. They looked exactly like running water. Had they foretold Mary's plan? Had she drowned herself? It seemed extremely likely. Drowned herself? At eighteen? Only a couple of years older than me. Suddenly unnerved, I jumped off the rock and hurried home.

That night, the awful anguished wailing came again, only this time I was frightened. I ran to the door, pulled it open and called out into the darkness:

"Who's there? Who is it?"

As well as this echo, a different one, intertwined with mine, came back, resounding off all four walls. It said

"Mary.....Mary.....Mary."
And I saw the brilliant marsh of white ahead of me. Hypnotised, I walked mechanically towards it. It seemed to shimmer and dance away from me. Slowly, it whispered: "Follow......me."

Crow

You scorn me
A black shadow
of the day,
A ragged breath
of stagnant air,
The undertaker
of the natural
world.
I pick the bones of animals
After loitering in a ditch,
waiting for the kill
From your gleaming Mondeos.
Yet I am just another bird,
Just surviving
Another low-paid road sweeper.

Beth Robinson (Nelson Thomlinson)

Cue Cumbria

Lonely Sultan Invents Time Machine

Matthew Cannon
(John Ruskin)

A new invention from the man who brought us wind powered submarines and a blow up dart board, Sultan Vinegar. I asked him what drove him to design this amazing invention. He replied:

"I design these inventions because I am lonely and I want a wife. I tried committing suicide once by jumping out of my bedroom window because I was so lonely. Fortunately I live in a bungalow."

He claims he has gone back in time to get Naomi Campbell (film star) to live in Saudi Arabia and to be his wife. NATO have currently put up a bid for copy. As well as Gareth Southgate who plans to go back to Euro 96 to change that missed penalty.

As Sultan Vinegar is extremely rich you would think it would be very easy for him to get a wife but his grotesque eating habits and excess wine drinking have made him look exactly like Jabba the Hut. Also his recent experiments have ridiculed him further.

His subs were swept away by the current and his dart board was a disaster due to the fact that every time you threw a dart, it popped.

"The side effects from the time machine are minimal," he said. "And the trial run with the hamster was a great success. I am sure it's leading a very happy life in the 16th century."

Please Mum!

Cue Cumbria

Sarah Mannix
(St. Aidan's)

For Christmas I want a Barbie doll
I want a Barbie doll like Jemma's.
Mum?
For Chistmas I want a Barbie doll like Jemma's
Will you tell Santa Mum?
Please Mum,
tell Santa I want a Barbie doll like Jemma's.
Santa will know what they are, won't he?
Oh please mum, tell him now!
Can you ring him up?
Tell him I want a Barbie doll like Jemma's
Mum?

Mum get up now! Look at this big present under the tree!
Ugh! Yuck!
I didn't want a Barbie doll, I wanted a beenie toy!
Mum!

Cue Cumbria

Men

Shirley-Anne Batey (Samuel King's)

Football
Drink
Sex
(That's it)

Where's the remote?
When's my tea?
Make us a cuppa
(That's it)

Side of the couch
Five O'clock
Make it yourself
(That's it)

They forget anniversaries
They're useless at housework
And looking after the kids
What are men for?

They go out to work
Fetch in the money
They father our children
And they're flat out under the car

Men will be men
Some way we'll love them
And keep them clean
What are men for?

Magical Reality

Elaine Capstick
(Settlebeck)

Abracadabra, tap, tap, tap,
Help me pull a rabbit out of my hat,
Cards, rabbits, top hats and tails,
Illusions,
Tricks play mind games,
Illusiveness overpowers
Steals reality,
Small insignificant tricks,
Creating wonder,
Mystification,
Making the brain work,
Opening your mind to new ideas
The trick's so persuasive,
Making you think,
Is reality questionable?

The Speeling Test
by Stewart Wardlaw
(Samuel King's)

Every Tuesday at 10 o' clock in the morning we have a speeling test. The teacher hands out small pieces of paper and you put your name on top. You see I'm dyslexic and I dread the speeling tests. Here comes the first word DIFFICULTY, how do you speel
DIFFICULTY, let me think, Mrs D, Mrs I, Mrs FFI, Mrs C, Mrs U, Mrs LTY, that's it, DIFFICULTY.
What! - everybody else is on number 7. I hate speeling!

Friends So Far
(A Sketch)

Samantha Tatters
(Whitehaven)

REBECCA	Louise, do you fancy Phillip?
LOUISE	What, Phillip? That is such a stupid idea. course I don't. That's just, *(pause)* just, *(pause)* just yuk. You're joking aren't you?
REBECCA	No, I'm not kidding. He really fancies you, he won't shut up about you. He says he dreams about you and all sorts, he's even written *Phillip and Louise* on his English folder.
LOUISE	Well, I suppose *(pause)* I mean, he *could* be - erm - that is, kinda alright, I suppose
REBECCA	You fancy him don't you.
LOUISE	No! Well - erm - kinda he's, OK, I do, just don't tell anyone.
REBECCA	Yeah, `OK. *(Pause)*. Look, I've gotta go and do something, see you soon, yeah?
LOUISE	Yeah, I'll go and see Dave and Andy or what ever.

(Rebecca goes to find Phillip)

REBECCA	Phillip - erm - what do you think of Louise?
PHILLIP	How do you mean?
REBECCA	I mean, do you fancy her?
PHILLIP	Course I don't - you must be kidding! I'd never fancy her, ever. Why?
REBECCA	Just that she fancies the pants off you. She's always talking about you. She has dreams about you. She's even written *Louise loves Phillip* on her geography book.

PHILLIP	Really?
REBECCA	Would I lie to you?
PHILLIP	Well, you never know.
REBECCA	No, I mean it, she really does.
PHILLIP	Well - er - I mean -
REBECCA	You mean, you *do* fancy her?
PHILLIP	Well - yeah.
REBECCA	Ask her out then.
PHILLIP	No!
REBECCA	Why not? You just said you fancy her. and she does fancy you.
PHILLIP	Yeah - OK, I'll ask her out.

(Phillip, Rebecca and Louise)

REBECCA	Hey, Louise, look who I've found.
LOUISE	Hi Rebecca *(pause)*. Hi, Phillip.
PHILLIP	Hi
REBECCA	I'll - er - leave you two alone then.
PHILLIP	Louise - will you - er - go out with me?
LOUISE	Yes, of course.

(Later)

REBECCA	What did you say then?
LOUISE	I - er - said yes.
REBECCA	Good on ya! Now I just need a boyfriend myself.

(End).

Cue Cumbria

The Founder of the Name Wigton
Wignal, Tony (1678-1739)

Eleanor Wakefield (Nelson Thomlinson)

Tony Wignal was an arrogant, upper-class man who was also extremely handsome. His blonde, straight waist-length hair (some said he had it ironed) captured female attention from throughout the county of Cumbria.

One day Wignal was walking through the main street of Hairtown (now Wigton) and found that he was being applauded by the townspeople. By asking one of the many farmers in the town, Wignal discovered that he had been awarded the status of Mayor of Hairtown (although this was only because the women were attracted to him).

As the first successful Mayor (others had left the town for various unknown reasons), the town was renamed WIG(nal)TON(y) - Wigton.

Wignal designed many things including the first textile factory in Wigton, He was taking part in the opening ceremony when his long locks got caught in a machine. Unfortunately, his hair was cut - there was no other way. This caused huge uproar - without his hair Wignal was ugly. He became infamous and his name lives on.

Cue Cumbria

The Worm

Kimberley Waite
(Nelson Thomlinson)

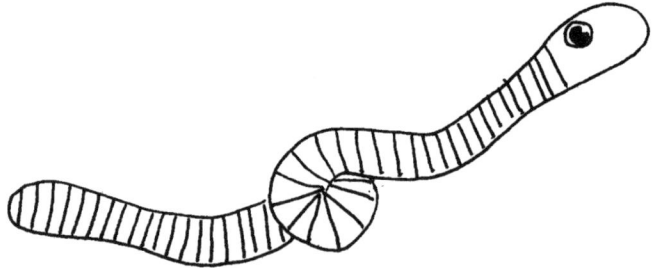

A thing to be tied in knots
by the fingers of impudent children.
A thing to be sliced in half
So I live two short lives

A poor thing torn from my home
by some insolent robin or wren;
Swallowed like a piece of spaghetti
Never to be seen again.

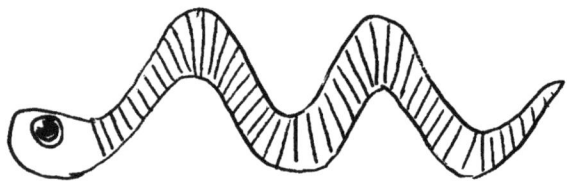

I've Been to the Dentist

James Kirby (St. Aidan's)

Are my teeth shiny
Do they gleam?
Please inform me
Before I scream.

Can you see the whiteness
Can you see them glow?
Come a little closer
I won't bite you know.

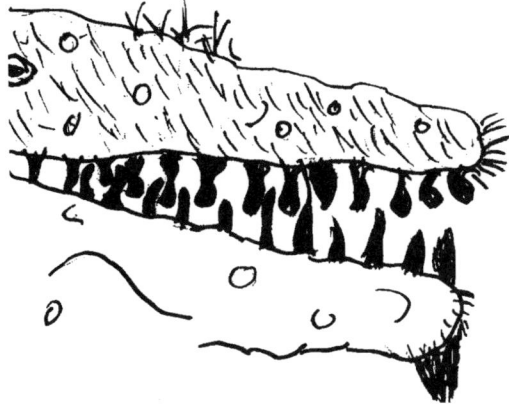

Come closer still my friend
I've already had my lunch
I'm full. I couldn't manage
Another crunch or munch.

You're close enough to see now
Relax. You're safe. Please smile.
One bite. One gulp. One swallow
OOPS! Never trust a crocodile.

Cue Cumbria

Dead Man's Party
(extract)

Terri
McCrickerd
(St.Joseph's)

The huge mansion's walls were worn with age. The faint glow from the setting sun cast long shadows over the men as they unloaded the wooden boxes.

Standing in the middle of the courtyard, Alex gave his orders. He watched eagerly as the boxes were mounted in accordance with his commands.

Once the boxes were in place, Alex approached them reverently.

"It's wonderful, isn't it?", he breathed.

"Yeah, it's a big pile," one of them drawled. "Can't wait to tell my friends. They don't have a pile this big."

Alex rolled his eyes and sighed. "Dean my boy, you don't have any friends to tell."

Dean gritted his teeth. "Well then, tell us what it is."

Sitting in her front room, Janna took another sip of her herbal tea as she watched the news on the TV unfold.

"The thirteen boxes were unearthed early yesterday morning near the new housing estate," the news announcer was saying.

"Although their present whereabouts is unknown, we do have these pictures."

Janna's throat went dry as the pictures flashed onto the screen. Her lips were dry as she whispered, "He's back."

"Thousands of years ago, demon Kistoss was brought forth to rid the world of the plague of humanity," Alex sermonised. "But a clan of goody-two-shoes gypsies trapped him into the stone form inside these boxes."

He moved forward and motioned for two of his men to move in.

"It will not however be able to use its own form for a number of hours. It will be able to use someone else's." He turned his back to the boxes.

"Boys."

With great care, two of the men inserted their crowbars into the sides of the boxes. With a groan, the front panel fell to the floor and Kistoss stood there in all its vile glory.

Its flesh was leathery and cracked, its face broad and chunky. It was enormous, crudely put together as if there had been no need for niceties or details. An elaborate dagger protruded from its chest.

"Let me guess" Dean said. "Someone pulls out the knife, the demon finds a host, and wackiness ensues.

Alex reached out for the dagger, and gripping the hilt, pulled it free.

Ward 14
by Stefenie Anderson
(Nelson Thomlinson)

A naked striplight burns;
Eyes like bloodhounds;
Mourning their own fate

The days when they fed us;
Forgotten

Cue Cumbria

Mummy Said

Amy Henderson
(Settlebeck)

Mummy said it would be fun
But I think it's scary
Sat in the big blue chair
That moves when a man pushes a button
He looks like a monster
With his funny white thing over his face
I can see his tools
The ones that poke around in your mouth
One is a spinning creature
Wanting to steal part of my tooth
Teachers tell us not to steal
I think the creature is bad
It smells funny in here
It makes me feel ill
Mummy says don't be silly and lie still
It smells yucky
Like cleaning stuff Mummy uses down the sink
Jimmy said he'd been here
He called it the tooth doctor
I don't like the man looking in my mouth
When I start to cry
He shouts and tell me to open wider
When he stops playing with my teeth
He plays pretend
He makes me think that he is nice.

Cue Cumbria

Hoover Mania

Jo Sedgwick
(Settlebeck)

Go!
Into the living room
over the edge of the carpet, bump
round the sofa...
what a mess!
Sweet wrappers, newspapers, soil and grass
Help someone please, I'm choking!
HELP! I'm dying *(cough, cough)*.
Cleared it
That hideous spider, all hair and legs, uhhh!
Back to the dining room
under the pool table, behind the piano
no! I haven't got all the dust!
On through the kitchen
stop for a rest.
Uh, she's caught me again
time to go!
Through the little room
trainers *(they smell like mould)*
PE bags *(ten times worse)*
hockey sticks, coats
What's this tasting like....like -
washing powder!
Come on, upstairs
Oh no, not back *under* the stairs!
I've only been out ten minutes!
You can't do this!
It's awful, it's inhoover!
You'd better let me out again soon!

Cue Cumbria

A Conflict of Powers
(extract)

**Steven Gibson
(Nelson Thomlinson)**

I had been dragging myself along the rough, coarse grass of the Yamasokoto plain for an hour towards Hirisami, when I heard noises amongst the forest which lay nearby. I felt like an escaped prisoner of war, and I was so fearful of capture that I laid face first in the middle of a group of grossly disfigured soldiers and feigned death.

As I lay there with my eyes tightly screwed shut, I imagined the soldiers hiding in the bushes, stifling laughter as they waited for me to move and give myself away. I could see in my mind the mangled faces of the dead warriors leering at me and laughing at my terror. I found myself close to delirium there on the edge of the dark, shadowy forest, but still my terror kept my mouth shut.

When at last I dared to stir I found I could not go on. My wounds had become badly infected and puss and blood gushed from them like water from a spring. I was so overcome with hunger and thirst that I had started to eat my clothing and drink my own blood. With every minute that passed my condition deteriorated further. I had lost all hope and lay on the edge of the forest cursing Major Gray and babbling about the horrors I had seen.

I was so ill that I had lost the ability to manipulate my remaining senses, dulled though they were, and I was oblivious to all that went on in the world around me. So when the British regiments of Somerby on Trent and Northbury arrived, I didn't know and I didn't care.

When I next regained consciousness I was lying wrapped up in bandages on a stretcher inside a sick bay. All was quiet. Again I strained my eyes but still could not find a clue as to my location. The room was quite old and the walls were cracked in many places. The few items of furniture I could see were carpeted in a thin layer of dust, and looked as if they had not been used in a long time. In some places varnished wooden floorboards showed through the ageing carpet, and above me people had crudely tried to repair the crumbling ceiling.

The room was in a state of disrepair, and the shadows cast by the few objects that lay strewn across the room added to the oppressive air of the place. I started at every creak and groan of the rickety wooden bed, and shivered with fright at every noise that penetrated the wall of this dreary sick room that I was in.

At last the first golden rays of the sun filtered through the grimy little windows of my lodgings and I was filled with hope that I could finally discover where I was being housed. But even with light to aid my search I could still uncover no definite evidence to support me being in the possession of either the British or the Japanese army. It was another hour or so of intense boredom before I heard footsteps leading up to the solid oak door of my room. As the door swung slowly inward I waited with bated breath knowing that now at last I would find out who my captors were. At last the man whose footsteps I had heard only moments ago strode into the room.

I knew this man was British, and as he entered the squalid little chamber which was my home, I saluted him and thanked him for saving my life.

"Hello", he said after I had finished thanking him. "My name is Commander Scott Welton of the Somerby-on-Trent Regiment, England. I understand that you are General Antoine

Cue Cumbria

de Bec, one of the last remaining survivors of the 17th Salbrose Regiment".
"That is correct", I replied.
"We have heard accounts of the battle from other soldiers who survived and what one person in particular told us is very disturbing. Let me put it clearly. You have been accused of being responsible for, and bringing about the murder of, 203 members of the 17th Salbrose Regiment and the injury of eleven other members of the company named. Do you admit to committing this despicable act of treachery and betrayal?"

Untitled
by Paul Wren
(Alfred Barrow)

I wish I could fly
Jump off buildings
Never die

The Pen

Lisa Doran (St. Joseph's)

Pulled out of the cold, dark drawer,
My life has purpose once more.
I am here to write her words,
Upon a blank sheet.
Her beautifully poised hands
Grasp my polished exterior.
As she writes of love unrequited,
My life source trickles across the page
Like blood from a broken heart.
I continue to bleed in silence;
My dark inside becomes clearer.
I feel the last drops of life drain away,
As her poem comes to a close,
And she signs her name.

Cue Cumbria

Asthma

Joanna Mottershead (Nelson Thomlinson)

...is like the sea;
Sometimes quiet, blue, calm,
That one might mistake it for the sky,
See blue in black, find birds in silence and
The struggle for the air.

Sometimes rough and stormy,
Fighting - playing
With life. My life. Your life.
Huge, catastrophic waves -
Like wafts of air
Filling empty lungs amd minds.

...is like the sky;
Blue, singing and still.
Peaceful, quiet, contented.
Just so many stars.

But you'll never know when
The clouds might come,
Pour down rain from tempests
Of rage.
Gasping
With the wind.

...is like a simile;
Just so many
Words
Ideas
Breaths

Struggles
Sighs before you win.

Or it wins.
It depends -
On how fresh the air is.
On how many scores of things you have to live for.
On how much will power you have.

And whether you can sit back and watch it win.

And Finally........
Claire Mattinson
(Nelson Thomlinson)

Darkclouds,
cold winds,
icy ground,
buckets of rain.
Welcome to Cumbria!

Cue Cumbria

The New Dictionary

The lingo of tomorrow!

As supplied by pupils of:
Samuel King's School, Alston, Whitehaven School, St. Joseph's RC School, Workington, Nelson Thomlinson School, Wigton

A

Amulokeob*(n)*   A hairless colourless cheetah found in Canada

Appopop*(n)*   Latin for money-making popcorn

B

Benraggle*(n)*   A house with no roof

Blumdan*(n)*   Cake of boiled eggs, pigs stomach, and prunes

Blut*(n)*   A spelling mistake

C

Chikkackakka*(n)*   The sound of a train

Coopoodifil*(n)*   Chemical like chlorophyl; turns plants to pigeons

Cootyboo*(n)*   Nice looking girl or boy

Cowswinkle*(n)*   A cow in pyjamas that runs through the town

Crample*(n)*   An elephant that does acrobatics in pyjamas

D

Dodilly*(n)*   A shirt worn while brushing hair off goldfish

Doomdeado*(n)*   A gun that fires burnt pies

Dwangle*(n)*   A large cabbage full of rats' testes

The New Dictionary

E

Eloquity*(n)* A talkative monkey
Erunk*(n)* A funky disco dancer

F

Fidspids*(n)* Glow in the dark spiders, £2.99 from ASDA
Flermintruck*(n)* A popular name for a pet flea
Flooby*(n)* A small cuddly animal that only eats cabbage
Fongshoparalmorkingk *(adj)* Short, to the point
Fromper*(v)* To run around with cheese & tomato on head
Funkatabulouse*(n)* A machine making 70s bellbottoms
Fwick*(n)* The study of pandemonium in bricklayers

G

Gangoe*(n)* A capsized canoe
Garankifin*(n)* A revolutionary car engine fuelled on old socks
Garolfank*(n)* A German hat for dogs
Gnawbrads*(n)* Children cartoon characters
Goningle*(v)* To eat piggishly

The New Dictionary

H

Himbright *(n)* — Plant in the Andes that sings in perfect English

Hodgick *(adj)* — Formal term to describe the opposite of logic

Hurchagill *(n)* — Red-finned fish that lives under volcanoes

I

Ilojokise *(n)* — An Icelandic jug

Ingleyzoo *(n)* — A person frantic about homework

J

Janovian *(n)* — A flash of lightning under the sea

Jumblebump *(n)* — third rate potato

K

Kalovne *(n)* — The language of the Arctic

Kero *(n)* — A type of ancient Egyptian moth

Ketick *(n)* — A small creature, described as "a flea of a flea"

L

Laponzer *(v)* — To kick old people heftily on the shins

Lenifew *(n)* — air too many thoughts on any subject

Lolipopxipoopx *(n)* — The sound of an opera singer on the loo

Lurpa *(n)* — Regurgitated supper

The New Dictionary

M

Mammalamma(n)	An animal with one leg
meniwomb(n)	Sexual transplant of mushroom spores
Mewniopy(n)	A place at Beamish
Minicularation(v)	Cleaning of septic eyelids
Mip(n)	Just-found Shakespeare play on alcoholic woman
Moltlomp(n)	A volcano that erupts baked beans
Morisunky(n)	An underwater flea

N

Nurning(v)	To stand in a swimming pool and snog

O

Orindachoochoo(n)	A two-wheeled train

P

Pamplehorner(n)	A horn to wake venus flytraps
Poshel(n)	A boil got after wrestling with alligators
Postel(n)	A chair too small for the table
Psad(n)	The Leader of the "Rubber Duck is God" cult

R

Racadical(n)	A farmer's dance performed on a pig's back
Ruggle(n)	A fight with a hotdog
Ryscoff(n)	A new flavour of cheesy crisps

The New Dictionary

S

Scazel(v)	To steal a goldfish by sucking it into a Hoover
Scubicals(n)	An instrument used to scrub behind toenails
Scurp(n)	A small hole in a badger's left eyebrow
Shomber(a)	Sad, and needing to be alone in the sea
Skiddywoody(v)	To slip on someone else's phlegm
Sklashop(n)	A strawberry meringue, dropped
Slammic(n)	A rap-star poltergeist that slaps baboons
Slundizz(v)	To surf in muddy water
Smollivos(adj)	Term used for object covered in chocolate
Solentishtish(v)	To have a custard pie put in your face
Splap(n)	Sound of cow hitting hind legs with tail
Squibbledegibblewdigoo(n)	Chewing gum in the mouth too long
Ssocasop(n)	Ancient form of writing used by Gaelic chiefs
Sturshunkle(n)	A forgotten school lunch sandwich

T

Techoratic(n)	A disco diva
Telephiphany(v)	To be scared of mobile 'phones
Tiglen(n)	A blue tiger that lives underground
Tintanoodlepanikala(n)	thin tube for unblocking toilets

The New Dictionary

Tittlebumble*(n)* A deodorant for bees
Totorum*(n)* A deformed ant
Triarite*(v)* To swim in treacle with a cake on your head
Twick*(n)* Powerful stain remover. Bought in packs of 72

W

Wabonerise*(v)* To talk endlessly about milk chocolate
Wazzle woff*(n)* A bad fart
Wessel*(n)* A book written by a monkey
Whatabilly*(n)* A ghost that's forgotten it's dead
Wincannyetoe*(n)* A large tree grown to hide an elephant

Y

Yimyamyoo*(n)* A biscuit that sings and dances
Yodderers*(n)* Crotchless trousers worn by Swiss yodellers

Z

Zebiolee*(n)* Egyptian dance performed by one-eyed cats
Zizzer*(n)* The thruster of a flying milk-bottle
Zolf*(v)* To race a snail

The following people participated in the Cue Cumbria project:

Alfred Barrow School, Barrow-in-Furness

Teacher:
Martin Plant

Pupils:
Hannah Cleasby
Rachel Grennell
Nicola Hall
Gemma McCowen
Anna-Alicia Parker
Paula Price
Claire Shaw
Katie Staunton
Gemma Staunton
Rachel Thomas
Laura Waite
Amy Wakefield
Paul Wren

John Ruskin School, Coniston

Teachers:
Ron Creer and Sue Sykes

Pupils:
Philip Baxter
Michael Bottomley
Matthew Cannon
Beth Dodd
Mary-Anne Evison
Martin Gallagher
Ben Grigg
Toby Hine
Patrick Isherwood
Jenny Kruger
Tom Smith

Nelson Thomlinson School, Wigton

School Librarian:
Claire Crone BA.ALA

Pupils:
Stefenie Anderson
Steven Gibson
Charlotte Liversidge
Claire Mattinson
Claire Millican
Joanna Mottershead
John O'Connor
Beth Robinson
Hannah Robinson
Claire Stewart
Kimberley Waite
Eleanor Wakefield

Samuel King's School, Alston

Teacher:
Jean M. Hill

Pupils:
James Alderson
Roderick Allen
Shirley-Anne Batey
Jacki Best
Jessica-Anne Burt
Alice Horrocks
Nicola McGarr
Imogen McGarvie
Vincent Peart
Laura Robson
Polly Smith
Stewart Wardlaw

St. Aidan's County High School, Coniston

Teacher:
Connie Jensen

Pupils:
Craig Bell
Louise Bell
Jennifer Boyd
Lynsey Galloway
Michael Johnstone
James Kirby
Davey Liddle
Thomas Little
Sarah Mannix
Paul Moralee
Thomas Prince
Gavin Routledge
Hannah Shepherd
Clare Stewart
Louise Wilson

St. Joseph's RC School, Workington

Teacher:
Anne Horrocks
Parent:
Christine Hadfield

Pupils:
Gabrielle Connor
Lisa Doran
Elizabeth Fye
Toni Gilmore
Clare McKay
Martyn Metcalfe
Terri McCrickerd
Gemma Park
Alexander Stewart
Kimberley Swinburne
Stephanie Roe
Hannah Trohear

Settlebeck High School, Sedbergh

Teacher:
Sally Ingham

Pupils:
Jayne Calvert
Elaine Capstick
Caroline Haigh
Amy Henderson
Ashley Iveson
Roxanne Kliszat
Joanne Sedgwick
Tom Swannick
Amy Symonds
Lindsey Telfer
Jessica Thompson
Beth Timson
Nick Wright

Whitehaven School, Whitehaven

Teacher:
Caroline Dunn
Librarian:
Sheila Ferguson

Pupils:
Natalie Craig
Emma Crowe
Caroline Eden
Katie Fairhill
Aimee Henry
Lynsey Jones
Amy Lawrence
Rachel McAlone
Samantha Tatters

About the Editors

SANDRA GLOVER is a qualified teacher and author of children's novels published by Anderson Press and Corgi. Her books include *'The Nowhere Boy'*, *'Breaking the Rules'* and *'The Girl Who Knew'*. Sandra was born in Manchester and now lives in Cumbria with her husband and three children.

PETER MORTIMER is a poet, playwright and editor of IRON Press. He lives in Cullercoats on Tyneside. His latest book, *'Broke Through Britain - One Man's Penniless Odyssey'*, is from Mainstream. His latest play, *'Lower The Lake!'*, was produced in October 2000 by Theatre by the Lake, in Keswick, as part of the Millennium Festival.

Cue Cumbria

Cue Cumbria

Cue Cumbria